WISDOM
IS THE BEGINNING

A better life starts with Knowledge

LIFE INSIGHT FROM HISTORICAL EXPERTS

BY GREGORY B. DAVIS

Wisdom is the Beginning: A better life starts with Knowledge. Life Insight
from Historical Experts. - First Edition

ISBN 978-1-7348643-3-5 (print)

Grateful

I'm grateful for my family. Always.

I feel I'm standing next to and on the shoulders of giants. The support of my family is vital to every part of my life and books. They've had my back since I was born and all the way to reading and rereading version after version of Wisdom is the Beginning. I'm humbled to be associated with such a loving and quality group.

Employ your time in improving yourself by other men's writings, so that you shall gain easily what others have labored hard for.

—Socrates, Greek philosopher

Table of Contents

Hello,

My name is Gregory B. Davis. I have a real passion for personal growth and learning in my life, but most importantly I enjoy helping others and seeing them advance in their life.

I am very fortunate to come from a family that believes personal growth is important.

They started to study and attend personal growth workshops and author lectures in the late 1970s. In 1983 my grandmother founded a seminar. The name has changed since then but it is still alive today.

I'm deeply thankful to play my part in it and lead the seminars. Having the great luck and opportunity to be around people who choose to grow keeps me sharp; I have surely seen and learned that everyone has the power within to create a successful life on their own, starting **today**.

By working with people closely and benefiting from my family's knowledge and experience, I've come to writing this book (this is my second book, my first book is: *Fight or Flight! Make better decisions to enjoy your life*).

I believe that every experience has been lived at some point in history and such knowledge is available to us, to not only make it through challenging times but also to come out of it stronger and more prepared to face the next test in our path.

It is exactly that notion that makes the core of these pages. I truly believe life is too short to learn every life lesson by ourselves, so gaining knowledge from others is key. I am proud and excited to contribute to the collective knowledge by passing on *Wisdom* so we can grow; here I present my work and research hoping that you take the knowledge and make slight changes in your life that will pay big dividends forever more.

"True life is lived when tiny changes occur."
—Leo Tolstoy, Russian writer

Introduction

We all have ambitions to leave a lasting influence. It might be through our work, children, science, media, politics, or many other fields. While these aspirations are alive as we move forward through life, we must prepare ourselves and pick ourselves up from our life's challenges. The most impactful and lasting influence on the world that we can leave is to become mentally healthy and strong. This, in turn, will impact our lives, allow us to face challenges, and support those around us. It breeds more love and health in every interaction by facing difficult situations and challenges instead of avoiding or delaying pain or fear.

We will all face challenges in life, and we can choose to see all that happens as beneficial, and as creating wisdom. We will deal with them in different manners. I believe that life is entirely too short to learn all of life's lessons by ourselves, therefore, in order to have the most successful life possible, we must learn some of those lessons from others.

The key to a successful life, and the goal of this book, are to: learn from others **before** life's obstacles are encountered, to consider another point of view when facing a challenge, and improve your mindset on how you think about what you face.

> "We come altogether fresh and raw into several stages of life, and often find ourselves without experience, despite our years."
> —Francois de la Rochefoucauld, French writer and memoirist

Where did I obtain the information about how to face these challenges? I looked back as far as I could in time and gathered quotes from life's greatest thinkers. Some names you'll know: Socrates, Lao Tzu, and Leonardo da Vinci. Plus I've added some not so well known names, such as Plutarch, Friedrich Koenig and many others. Finally, I've added input, in bold, from my experience of leading personal growth workshops and difficulties that I've faced.

Often it is greatly beneficial for us to take a step back and rest when we are facing a challenge. It gives us a break and allows us to see new information and, hopefully, a new solution. This book will give you new information to face challenges you are currently confronting and perhaps to see the opportunity in a different way.

Luckily, life teaches everyone lessons. Also, unfortunately it teaches us again and again until we learn the intended lesson. This book is meant to give you a head start in learning those lessons so that you can face them and overcome them with greater ease.

> "Self-knowledge comes from knowing other men."
> —Johann Wolfgang von Goethe, German poet

Opening Story

The main reason Marie Curie (Marie Sklodowska Curie) is famous in the world is due to her having obtained **two** Nobel Prizes in **two** different fields, but I've chosen to cite her in this book for a slightly different reason. Looking beyond her prizes, she is an outstanding example of an individual and a family who represent the (generational passing and) use of *Wisdom* for the betterment of the world and then passed it along to others, including her daughters, so that, in turn, they could improve it as well. Her family, ancestors and descendants, represent true heritage of knowledge.

This is the exact concept behind *Wisdom is the Beginning*: to gain and use knowledge from all sources available so that in whatever life brings you, you excel and, in turn, you share what you've learned with others.

Marie was surrounded by knowledge of the sciences her entire life; her parents were both teachers, her father of math and physics, and her mom ran a boarding house before Marie was born. Additionally, one of her grandfathers was a respected teacher. After reading about her life, I conclude this heritage influenced her at a young age to face adversity and excel. An example of this is that she made an agreement with an older sister to help her pay her university fees if the support was returned a few years later when it was time for her to attend.[1]

As humans, we face difficulties on the road of life. Marie, who faced many well documented adversities in her life, including sexism every step of the way, proved to be a history-making and world-changing scientist through it all. For our purposes, we have ample opportunity to learn from Marie's life and challenges.

Some of the life challenges she faced in her youth were: losing her mother at the age of ten; she could not attend University in Warsaw because she was a woman; also, the family faced hostilities due to their political views. Once she reached adulthood and moved to Western Europe, she experienced xenophobia; the death of her husband early in their marriage; and health concerns due to her experiments.[2]

How do you face all of the above and still become a history-making scientist? Marie had uncommon intellect and drive and the wisdom of her family and husband to

---

1   Biography Marie Curie. Biography.com. The Biography.com website. Accessed June 2020. www.biography.com/scientist/marie-curie.

2   Des Jardins, Julie. "Madame Curie's Passion". Smithsonian Magazine. Accessed June 2020. www.smithsonianmag.com/history/madame-curies-passion-74183598/

face all in her path. I find this quote from her husband, Pierre, proof of this:

> "It would be a beautiful thing, to pass through life together hypnotized in our dreams: your dream for your country, our dream for humanity; our dream for science."
> —PIERRE CURIE, NOBEL PRIZE WINNER

Marie's studies and career highlights were awe inspiring:

- Became the first female faculty member of Éole Normale Superieure
- Awarded a doctorate degree from the University of Paris
- Discovered radioactivity
- Announced the existence of new elements: polonium and later radium
- Worked to develop x-rays
- Obtain professorship at University of Paris (first female)
- Founded Curie Institutes in Paris and Warsaw

As mentioned, she won her first Nobel Prize in Physics for her part in the research of radiation and was the first woman to win a Nobel Prize. A few years later she won her second Nobel prize in Chemistry; at that moment she became the first person to win a prize in two fields.

One of the most powerful parts of her story is that

she passed on her wisdom and knowledge to her daughters; her oldest, Irene Curie, became a chemist, physicist and politician and also won a Nobel Prize for her work in artificial radioactivity.

1898	1903	1906	1911	1935
Earns Physics degree University of Paris & discovered polonium/ radium	Wins first Nobel Prize - Physics[3]	First female professor University of Paris	Wins second Nobel Prize - Chemistry[4]	Irene Curie (Marie's daughter) wins Nobel Prize[5]

The take-away from Marie Curie's story is that *Wisdom is the Beginning* of abundance for you and your family which can be passed along generationally to face the toughest times and can be used to better one's life and the entire world. While your passion may not be in the sciences, *Wisdom* can be found and passed along in any area of life.

---

3   Biographical. NobelPrize.org. Nobel Media AB 2020. Accessed June 2020. www.nobelprize.org/prizes/physics/1903/marie-curie/biographical/.
4   ibid.
5   Biography Marie Curie. Biography.com. The Biography.com website. Accessed June 2020. www.biography.com/scientist/marie-curie.

Wisdom is the Beginning

Life's Challenge: Consider for a moment the amount of knowledge that is available to us in the world. Consider the historical books, research papers, articles, insight from our elders, friends with similar life experiences, ebooks, plus many others. The sheer quantity is mind blowing and empowering (our answer is out there!). Wisdom is the beginning of how we will face challenges in our life. We can choose two paths—encounter the knowledge and wisdom all on our own or seek insight from those around us. We don't necessarily get to choose what challenges come our way, but we can choose how uncomfortable it is to make our way through those times.

> "Man arrives as a novice at each age of his life."
> —Nicolas Chamfort, French writer

Wisdom is the Beginning: I believe the ability and knowledge of the "group" to solve problems is much more powerful than by the individual. We can go alone through life, figuring out a way forward every step, and many do. However, what is the harm in learning the best way from others who've been there before us? It doesn't make us less of a person. I believe it is the wisest of us who seeks the knowledge of others. Hence "Wisdom is the Beginning" is the way forward to obtain a full life and face its challenges with knowledge and to gain more understanding.

> "Appreciation is a wonderful thing: It makes what is excellent in others belong to us as well."
> —VOLTAIRE, FRENCH WRITER

One of the biggest oddities for me in life is seeing that some people want to stay right where they are and refuse to consider that there could a better way. Life starts with broad openings to go and do what the mind and heart desire, but then as time passes slowly, the walls close in and desires and dreams are put aside, lost and given up. A life of flexibility and openness gives way to rigid ways of looking at things and closed mindedness. I'm not sure if they are tired, have given up on life, or are deeply hurt. If you find yourself there now, acknowledge that you don't have all the information about life and that there is an easier way to accomplish what is in front of you.

People sometimes appear to be happy when truly they are not, instead of using the energy to convince others of what they want to hide–imagine the life that can be created learning and then applying new knowledge to build a passion filled life.

"We are more interested in making others believe we are happy
than in trying to be happy ourselves."
—Francois de la Rochefoucauld, French writer and
memoirist

Who's in control of your thoughts? It does seem like
a strange question at first, however it is deeper than it first
appears. How much of your thoughts are controlled by
habit? What percentage of your thoughts are shaped by
past challenges or people have who hurt you? There are
many heavy influences on what you think and the reasons
you think the way you do.

You must take a step back and consider how to
influence your thoughts and what you think. There is a
better manner to approach life. The issue is not everyone
has the same knowledge. What you think of as common
sense does not to seem widespread in people's lives. Even
in Voltaire's time, it was an issue.

"Common sense is not so common."
—Voltaire, French writer

Once you acknowledge that you don't know
everything, and that there is likely a more productive
manner in which to approach life and the difficulties
within it, then the mind is open to learning that better
is possible. When you know better, you do better in life.
The biggest impediment to learning something new, or

approaching a challenge in a new way, is feeling that you know the answer or how it will work out.

> "What we achieve inwardly will change outer reality."
> —PLUTARCH, GREEK PHILOSOPHER

Problems in life occur externally and/or internally. When you work to solve an internal problem with an external solution, it cause you great frustration. Be clear on what type of problem you have and then approach it with potentially fruitful solutions. If at first you don't succeed at conquering the road block in your life, then seek new wisdom and do something different. The solution is there, someone has walked ahead of you and has the answer. Now you have to find your way.

Every man I encounter is better than me in at least one area of life. I have a lot to learn and I'd prefer to learn it from others and not have to learn everything myself. Learning for myself is incredibly enlightening and powerful. In addition, learning everything on my own is tiring and takes a lot of time and energy, plus it expands one's mind.

> "Learning never exhausts the mind."
> —LEONARDO DA VINCI, ITALIAN ARTIST, SCIENTIST
> AND ENGINEER

Either way there is a huge payoff to learning in life. Often there is an easy way and a hard way. You can get to the other side of the doorway by opening the door or breaking it down. Both will accomplish the same goal. Socrates challenged his fellow Greeks to think in a different way.

> "The unexamined life is not worth living."
> —SOCRATES, GREEK PHILOSOPHER

There is wisdom in these pages for you, to open your mind to new information and learning that there might be a better more productive manner to succeed at life. When you change your thoughts and thought processes, you'll change those challenges and succeed even in the face of failure.

Bottom Line for Wisdom is the Beginning: You will face many difficult challenges. How you view these challenges and the tools you use to face them will make a world of difference. In the first chapter on Failure, you will learn how it affects your life now and how it will, in a large way, dictate how you feel and experience life.

Failure

Life's Challenge: We will all experience **failure**.

At my words, "I've failed," the group around me cringes. People shift in their seats because those words take them to a place in their life when they've also not succeeded. The topics and areas are endless where those experiences can be encountered. For example, when we fail our family, we damage relationships over the long term. Maybe it is that we have our identity and ego wrapped with our careers, so that when we fail at work, or our business, it enters all areas of our life. The worst part of connecting our self-worth with our professions is that it sticks with us. We feel as though people can see our self-doubt when we enter a room, and that the side comments they make to others are about us and our past. We will never escape it!

In our culture, we have an interesting relationship with failure. People don't want to experience it in their personal or professional life, yet we all know it will happen, so we often root for the underdog and the individual who's failed and resurrected their career or business. However, we don't particularly want to walk that road ourselves. One of the biggest worries of all is the deep fear that we're not worthy of success. If we stop and give up, then failure is no longer possible. Certainly, once stopped, success is no longer possible either. Now we've set up the quandary; when we stop, there is no success or failure, and when we move forward, all is now possible, even failure until we reach success.

Wisdom is the Beginning: You must change your view on failure and give yourself a more well- rounded and healthy viewpoint.

For myself, I knew my first book would not make it on the bestseller list (it actually never left my computer's memory), however, I knew the experience of writing and learning would lead me to the next book and the next, which would encompass personal success. While failure will happen, and you will never be excited to experience it in your life, you can become more rewarded in life as a result of failure and use it to your advantage.

When it happens next, use the wisdom from history's greats to get back up and move forward. Stopping and giving up is not an option.

> "Do not fear mistakes. You will know failure.
> Continue to reach out."
> —Benjamin Franklin, founding father of US
> Declaration of Independence

Failure can be seen and experienced as the beginning of a new path or as a dead end. Seeing failure as a dead end is defeat, but if you experience it as a new beginning, or at worst a delay in the road to success, then value is created. In life, failure can only be avoided by internally dying by making the choice to say nothing, do nothing new, and be nothing.

Everyone will experience failure. At that point you have an important decision. Will you connect yourself to the failure and wear it as a badge your entire life (Look at me I failed; I'm a failure), or will you get back up and move forward and work towards a new badge (Look at me I failed, but now I'm a success)? It is possible to fail your way to success. Inventors often fail often before they find the solution.

"My great concern is not whether you have failed, but whether you are content with your failure."
—Abraham Lincoln, US President

Will you see your failures as successes learned, and get up and move forward with persistence? Nothing in the world is more powerful at changing failure into success as persistence.

When failure is seen as an end, then it is a painful part of you and your life. When you choose to change the manner in which you experience failure and look on the other side of the event, you can use it to increase your successes in life. If you throw it aside and put it in your past, then it will hurt forever. When you keep it with you, and use it to expand your experience in life, you become more capable and the failure becomes useful. You can choose to come to peace with it and make it part of your growth.

"Mistakes are the portals of discovery."
—JAMES JOYCE, IRISH NOVELIST AND POET

You either fail and stay down or get back up and use those life lessons to accomplish bigger more impactful life-goals for yourself in the future. You can choose not to live and do "nothing," but if you're reading this book, that is not a true choice for you. Unfortunately, there is no truly impactful and successful life without failure.

Think about someone in your life who you consider successful. What has that person achieved? We too often look at a successful person's life and see success and no failure, but this is a huge error because we are seeing a single point in life and not the road traveled that led to that point. When looking at a truly successful life, there is only failure until there is success upon success.

There are huge opportunities inside business organizations to change the viewpoint on failures/errors/delays. When you throw a "failure" aside and choose not to find the value in the lessons learned, you're losing a big opportunity.

As leaders in businesses, organizations you must challenge the default beliefs and adjust accordingly, from the top down. Additionally, in these circumstances, leaders have a key role in encouraging others and learning versus sweeping a failure under the rug. It will set the tone for the entire organization.

"I've not failed. I've just found 10,000 ways that won't work."
—THOMAS EDISON, US INVENTOR, BUSINESS MAN

Take a step back and consider that Failure is all mindset. At the point of failure, of course, we are disappointed, we knew there would be success at the end of the project and now there is not. Now is the vital point; what will you do at that moment? Will you see it as a failure forever more or change your point of view and know 1) what didn't work, or that 2) now you're more valuable, more experienced, and 3) you know what has a higher chance of working.

The younger you are, the more powerful this lesson can be. The sooner you realize you can pick yourself up after "failure" and grow stronger, the more successful your life and career will be. How many times will it take to reach success?

"Fall down seven times, get up eight."
—JAPANESE QUOTE

Failure can bring about positives in numerous ways. One key benefit might be for an individual to determine if this incident impacts a future course. If you choose to shift your project and life goals, then let it go and move on.

If you decide your future is to remain the same or on a similar path, then learn from the set-back, learn what didn't work and use it to move forward with more knowledge. The experience will be of use to you or someone in your life; all learnings are an asset.

> "The doer alone learneth."
> —Friedrich Nietzsche, German philosopher

When I speak to youth about failure, I beg them to go and fail and keep their sanity while it happens. That is a winner in life. Keep your peace of mind the next time you fail, and keep it in perspective.

The only true failure in life is a time when one completely gives up and chooses to play small. It is the saddest state. One day the individual will awake and realize what has happened and the poor decision that was made. One can only hope it is not the final day.

> "Every man is guilty of all the good he did not do."
> —Voltaire, French writer

Failures of the heart, with our key relationships, might be the most dangerous. When we fail professionally, we can fall back on our family and loved ones. When we fail in our family, it is much more difficult to fall back on our professions. While the two are interlinked for many, keep the home and nuclear family healthy and stable, for a weakened foundation is difficult to fix.

"Keep failure out of your heart."

The biggest, most powerful, distinction you must make is to separate the failure in the situation from the failure of your life. The biggest fear I have is not of living, but not putting forth my best. It is not true that a failure in an instant or event is attached to us in its entirety. It is understandable to have fears and fear of failure.

"Just because I fail doesn't mean I'm a failure."

Under no circumstance is failure an end state. The healthiest state of mind is: failure and success are not opposites; they are intertwined. Know that it will happen and know that you can change your viewpoint on the experience and create value.

Here is the final stretch for you and your life. See success as enjoyable; it is positive and will come into your life. Much more valuable for your life is failure because it teaches. You have a choice; you can experience failures in life, or you can fail life. That's the bottom line. If you choose to never fail in life while living, you've failed life by default.

Bottom Line for Wisdom is the Beginning: Celebrate your failures! Change your mindset and see every failure as a step closer to success in your life.

Wisdom is the Beginning Personal Activity: Identify three of your biggest failures in life (professional, personal, relationship, etc.) and decide:

1. Was it truly a failure or merely a setback or a redirect in life?
2. If you still view it as a failure, which quote from the chapter can you apply to bring some clarity to the situation?
3. What is your next step to create value from the situation and bring strength where there was failure?

Fear

Life's Challenge: We touched on the fear of failure in the previous chapter. In broader context, our fears in life will limit us. When we are not incredibly careful, our fears will run and ruin our lives. As children, we experienced the world as wide open, and our fears were few and far between. However, as we grow and age, the fears squeeze tighter and thicker. Fears can limit us and suck the joy out of life.

> "We promise according to our hopes and perform according to our fears."
> —Francois de la Rochefoucauld, French writer and memoirist

Fears lurk in all parts of our life, and when we tune in, we can see that they limit us in our relationships, careers, as parents, as friends, while investing, flying, and so on. They are a fact of life. The problem is not necessarily that we have fears (lots of them), it is how we allow them to impact our lives. The goal of this chapter is to acknowledge them in our life and then move through the fear by changing the way we view them in life.

"Step out in your faith and fear."

Fear is not an option in life, but how you react to them and define fear is an option.

Wisdom is the Beginning: I have a special place in my heart for Fear. I wrote an entire book on the topic: *Fight or Flight! Make better decisions to enjoy your life.* You must decide if you are in a fearful or dangerous situation. Fear is largely created in the mind and rarely beneficial. Danger is life or death, and you must deal with it as quickly as possible.

You must understand what you fear and choose to walk toward it. Choose to identify the triggers of the emotions and find a way to deal with the cause of the fear that is blocking you from becoming your best self. Walking away from your fear puts it in control of your life. Fears are learned (from parents and society largely), therefore they can be unlearned and transformed into something else.

"Do the things you fear and the death of fear is certain."
—Ralph Waldo Emerson, American writer

Fears that you've created in your mind of "what might happen" or focus on the "worst case scenario" are all too often never experienced, and you waste energy to avoid something that is not real. They rob of you of your fullest possible life. Fear and ignorance are tightly intertwined. Learn, learn, learn about your fears and life and you'll discover you are your worst enemy and that you limit your life far more than any other person or event.

The more power you give your fear, the more your life is limited. Dead at 50 years old and buried at 70.

> "Fear is pain arising from the anticipation of evil."
> —ARISTOTLE, ANCIENT GREEK PHILOSOPHER

Our head and brains are such powerful instruments. They lead us to great opportunities, big wins and successes. What leads us one way can lead us another way. You can fear your life away in your head. That is the reason we started with Failure and Fear as the two first chapters. They go hand in hand, and one can lead to the other and crescendo over time. Use this book to set your direction to success, not fear.

> "It is a queer thing, but imaginary troubles are harder to bear than actual ones."
> —DOROTHEA DIX, 19TH CENTURY AMERICAN ACTIVIST

Who is judged more harshly in the world? The person on their death bed who conquered nothing in life due to fear, or the person on top of the world? Two very different paths were taken. Without a doubt, both encountered numerous fears along the way. Perhaps many of the same fears with differing levels of impact on each person. Who was judged more harshly over their lifetime?

I suggest the person on top of the world will face more external verbal judgment. However, and more importantly, the voice in the person's head saying "you've wasted and feared your life away" is the harshest and loudest critic of them all.

"We can easily forgive a child who is afraid of the dark; the real tragedy of life is when men are afraid of the light."
—PLATO, GREEK PHILOSOPHER

Fears are simply made up tales you continue to tell yourself over and over again. You believe every word and the "bad guy" wins every time. The fairy tale will go on as long as you allow it. Unfortunately, if you continue to tell it, the story only grows and become more detailed and convincing. You must step out of the story in your head and live the fear for it to lose its power. At that point the big bad fear will become small.

"There are more things to alarm us than to harm us, and we suffer more often in **apprehension** than reality."
—LUCIUS ANNAEUS SENECA (SENECA THE ELDER)
[EMPHASIS IS MINE]

In the simplest of points of view, you can either chose

to grow or shrink in your life experiences. One afternoon of sitting on the couch watching mind-numbing TV has a minimal impact, but one week does have an influence, and one year of afternoon after afternoon has a larger effect. Your days make your weeks, which makes your year and then your life. If you put fear in the driver's seat, and sit on the couch day after day, then your life will become smaller and more narrow. How you do anything is how you do everything, until you make a conscious decision to change. Choose to move forward every day.

The best news of all is that your fears can lose their power as you move forward and expand in life. Growth is a powerful force. As you choose to learn and cultivate your experiences, you want more, and your weaknesses and fears shrink. At one point it could be a mental game to seek out fears and face them.

> "If you keep feeling a point that has been sharpened, the point cannot long preserve its sharpness"
> —Lao Tzu, Chinese philosopher

Once it starts, fear has the sharpest point, and can be built up in your mind and imagination if left unchecked. It is of the utmost importance to understand that it dulls immediately as a decision is made and action is undertaken.

> "Death is not the worst that can happen to men."
> —Plato, Greek philosopher

Death is a fact of life. We will examine it later in the book. Not living is a choice you make every day, out of fear.

As you may have noted with many of the Greats' quotes, it is not the fact that fears appear in life, but it is that people allow them to run their life instead of challenging them. The worst that can happen to people is that their fear runs and ruins their lives. When people allow this, it has a dramatic effect. As a man's life is draining away in the final days, his fears subside and it becomes clear that life never fully happened.

One must be intentional with time and life experiences. If you spend your days locked in fear, then your days will not be experienced in fullness. There is a lifetime of excitement and fulfillment waiting for you. Fully step into your experience feel the fears and find the joys.

"Everything you've ever wanted is on the other side of fear."
—GEORGE ADDAIR, REAL-ESTATE DEVELOPER IN POST-CIVIL WAR ATLANTA

Will you allow your life to be run and ruled by your fears or your dreams? It is your choice to run or ruin your life by where you focus. Life will go in the direction where the mind spends its time. Does it have the power position for you in the dark imagination? Or the part of you that knows the truth about who you are and what is important in its purest form?

"Life is to be entered upon with courage."
—ALEXIS DE TOCQUEVILLE, FRENCH ARISTOCRAT, DIPLOMAT,
POLITICAL SCIENTIST AND HISTORIAN

Furthermore, I suggest that, on the other side of our fears, lies our biggest dreams in life. Ponder for a moment the reason you haven't accomplished your dreams. On some level, there is a fear blocking your path. Also, the passion to move forward in life is like gasoline—we need it and it makes life worth it.

"The pleasures of love are always in proportion to our fears."
—STENDHAL, FRENCH AUTHOR

"PART OF WHAT I FEAR I CREATE IN MY LIFE."

Now when you can get to a point of self-awareness and strength, you have the opportunity to share your fears with others in your life. This action has the ability to 1) allow you to examine them in truth and obtain an outside opinion (they are rarely as controlling after they are spoken); and to 2) allow the other person to check out the validity of their own fears.

"YOUR GREATEST FEARS ARE MEANT TO BE SHARED."

When you become brave, vulnerable, and share your fears with those around you, then you instantly have the

41

opportunity to deepen relationships to give those around you the ability to share their fears too. It can be a profound bonding experience for the relationship. At first it can be overwhelming to share, however staying silent keeps the fear in control of your life.

Ask your fears a question: What are my options in this situation? And what does fear always respond? It often says, over and over, to stay in bed and play small in life, do nothing, shut down emotionally, verbally and physically.

Those who decide to speak openly about fears begin to gain control over the situation. Also, there is an opportunity to receive new information about the situation from a trusted companion. As long as fears are hidden away, they not only stay alive in you but grow in size over time.

> "To live life to the fullest, you must lose the attachment to your fears."

Fears move you away from something in your life and are very effective at their job. Your life will become fuller when moving toward something; your brain works best when it has a target. In short, fears are used to avoid, not obtain. This, in turn, leads to the question: Do you want to avoid life or obtain something?

Bottom Line for Wisdom is the Beginning: Fear is absolutely real (in your head), it will run your life (to nothingness) and will say "I told you so" on your deathbed.

"How very little can be done under the spirit of fear"
—FLORENCE NIGHTINGALE, PIONEER OF MODERN NURSING

Wisdom is the Beginning Personal Activity: What is your single biggest fear? How does it control you, and what cost do you pay to allow it to be in charge? How would your life be different if you released the fear?

Unhappiness: Happy vs. Unhappy

Life's Challenge: Happiness, the vaguest word we chase our entire lives.

Define happiness for yourself; it is a fruitful mental activity.

I ask people what they want more of in their lives and they say to be happier. Nice, but vague, to the point of becoming impossible to obtain. Once an individual refines or defines what they want to be happy being or doing in their life, they can become more fulfilled, excited, powerful, loving, and so on.

Too often, in our society, we have learned to look outwardly to fill up our happiness bucket. At this point in my life, I have learned that looking to others to make it happen is a worthless activity, because we can only become happier (over the long term) by starting inward with our quest for happiness.

Gregory B. Davis

"Happiness must start on the inside."

Happiness is not a final state; life is about peaks and valleys of emotions. Believing that you can simply climb the mountain of happiness and stay will only bring disappointment when you're heading down the back side. Life is happy and joyous at times, sad and painful at others. Focus your mind on the fact that life is unhappy, at times, and know that internally you create true happiness.

Wisdom is the Beginning: Magic fairy dust doesn't exist. Everyone would enjoy a quick "happiness" fix. One that is readily available, in unlimited supply and bringing no side effects. Alas it is only found in books and legends. If it is to be had, only you can make it so.

> "Happiness is a state of activity."
> —Aristotle, Ancient Greek philosopher

Be Do Have is a powerful tool to use to drive your life to a state of happiness. **Be** committed to **Do** what it takes so that you **Have** what you want in life.

Unfortunately, we are often caught up in the "Have" piece. If I had *x*, then I'd be happy. If I had that raise, car, relationship, and so forth, all would be good in my life forever more.

> "The only joy in the world is to begin."
> —Cesare Pavese, Italian poet

Then... we obtain "x" and it is not nearly as fulfilling as we expected while awaiting its arrival. The raise—the money was quickly spent. The new car smell fades and the car gets dirty. The new relationship is euphoric at first, then the realization settles in that the other is imperfect.

The simple act of obtaining the things we desire does not bring anything but momentary happiness. Big time, long term, deep happiness comes from us living in a place of working toward "having" not the result of obtaining "x."

"Happiness is not something ready made. It comes from your own actions."
—Dalai Lama, spiritual leader

Live in the act of planning and implementing your dreams; this will set you up for true long-term happiness. Once the dream comes true, it is like the cherry on top.

"We tend to forget that happiness doesn't come as a result of getting something we don't have, but rather of recognizing and appreciating what we do have."
—Friedrich Keonig, German inventor

Desiring the perfect happy life is a sure-fire way to create an unhappy state. When perfection is chased, it robs you of the glory of achieving the goal, in that once the goal is reached it is never acknowledged; you simply move on to the next goal or raise the bar of the last goal because it was "too low." Give yourself permission to celebrate your wins and key moments along the way.

It took me over four years to finish my first book *(Fight or Flight: Make better decisions to enjoy your life)*, and before it was published, I had *Wisdom is the Beginning* in the final steps to start the publication process. I'd decided to celebrate when my first book was sold, then I changed that to when I'd sold 100 copies. Then I thought, *Well how about when I have both books published; they are both so close.* The truth is that I felt comfortable drawing a lot of attention to myself. My perfectionism robbed me of the opportunity to celebrate a big win that took me years to obtain.

"THERE IS NO END STATE OF A PERFECT LIFE, ONLY THE EXPERIENCE THROUGH LIFE."

Aim for the passionate, happy, dream-filled moments. Understand there will be unfortunate and difficult moments up ahead. Once those come and go, continue to make more beautiful memorable moments. Nothing in life happens without commitment. There is no magic fairy dust, no prince or princess on a horse, no billion-dollar lottery around the corner. Expecting one to enter your life only creates more problems and unsatisfactory feelings. Enjoy life where it is right now.

No exterior force will bring you lasting happiness in life. It must be created from within yourself. In my experience, those who have decided that they are in control of how they experience what happens in life are the happiest. No one has the power to make you happy, only you have that power. You don't have control of everything in life, but you have control of what you do and what you believe about yourself and those events.

> "Very little is needed to make a happy life; it is all within yourself, in your way of thinking."
> —MARCUS AURELIUS ANTONINUS, ROMAN EMPEROR AND PHILOSOPHER

It is all within yourself, all within your control. When you acknowledge that happiness is self- generated and self-sustained, then you receive the greatest gift of all. Expecting others or objects to bring you happiness means that it can and will be taken away. What you give to yourself cannot be taken away. For if it starts to fade, you only need to refocus and the gift will return.

The trap is ugly; constantly looking outward to things will only leave you giving away your happiness. When you make the choice to believe that happiness is solely an exterior experience, you will chase it your entire life without fully obtaining.

Therefore, clarity as to the path that you walk fills you with joy.

> "Before we set our hearts too much upon anything, let us examine how happy they are who already possess it."
> —FRANCOIS DE LA ROCHEFOUCAULD, FRENCH WRITER AND MEMOIRIST

I love to use others' wisdom as my guide in my next steps. I look for and find those who are the happiest, most peaceful people, living life to the fullest that I know. Then I examine their lives. Are they the richest? Some yes, some no. Are they surrounded by loving relationships? Yes. Do they have passions in life? Yes. Do they have big houses? Not always. Then I can look at my ideals and see what area I can influence so that I can bring more of the emotions I want to my life.

> "We never live; we are always in the expectation of living."
> —Voltaire, French writer

Begin to understand what brings you personal and lasting "happiness," then focus on that. It brings more and more to life. An example from my life is reading and writing for pleasure. I grew up avoiding both due to Dyslexia. Only when I made the conscious decision in my mid-twenties to read for the simple enjoyment did I begin to understand how much happiness and joy it brought to my life. Writing and, more specifically, the passing along knowledge to others, I find fulfilling and purposeful.

Beware of the slippery slope of unhappiness, because it can grow and consume more of your life. The more you focus on your state of what you don't like and don't want, the more you receive of those states. It becomes your daily guiding light.

I've been presented with the idea that living a happy life is like listening to a favourite song. We don't wait for the final note to enjoy the song. This is what we are doing when we focus solely on the outcome of the situation. We enjoy the entire musical event—the notes, lyrics, environment and companionship. This makes the "Be" and "Do" the enjoyable part of life. The dream coming true, the last note is the cherry on top of a beautiful journey.

Bottom Line for Wisdom is the Beginning: Give yourself and your brain a target of defined happiness and you'll achieve... I have no doubt you'll obtain, but first gain clarity.

> "Happiness depends upon ourselves."
> —ARISTOTLE, ANCIENT GREEK PHILOSOPHEr

Wisdom is the Beginning Personal Activity: 1) Define *happiness* in your own words, and to the greatest detail. 2) You can choose to make new habits and focus on happiness and thankfulness. Journal three items that made you happy or thankful each day (in bullet points). Start your evening conversation with your family or friends about what was the best thing that happened to you or them during the day.

Problems

Life's Challenge: What we perceive as problems impact us all every day. Every moment they are waiting for us around all corners. We solve one and the next one enters.

Having problems are similar to having change in life, no matter how organized you are. No matter how lucky, no matter how hard you work, there is always another problem and more waiting up ahead. The key is to form a new mindset about problems and not experience them as draining. It is too easy to allow them to drain the joy out of life.

Wisdom is the Beginning: You have made a simple choice with life's problems and challenges. Blame something or someone, but the outcome is that nothing will change, and your problem will persist. The flip side of blaming is to take control of the situation and do your part in finding the solution. Then continue to search for the solution until it is found; there is no gain in choosing to be the victim.

"Every man has his secret sorrows which the world knows not;
and often times we call a man cold when he is only sad."
—HENRY WADSWORTH LONGFELLOW, AMERICAN POET

When we give into a life of unsolvable problems, we become sad. Life is full of problems, and as long as we experience them as unending, we experience a drained life that becomes sad.

The moment you see problems up ahead that are huge, complex, ugly and a bit frightening, they seem insurmountable. At that moment you have a choice—move toward it or stop. When you choose to stop, the problem becomes more complex, huge, ugly, frightening and insurmountable. When you chose to move toward it and face it, you begin to win. Life's problems rarely are as insurmountable as they appear to be from a distance, and they will never go away when you stop.

"Life is not a problem to be solved, but a reality to be experienced."
—SOREN KIERKEGAARD, DANISH PHILOSOPHER

Even though life has problems in it, life is not a problem. When people choose not to face them, often they engage in criticism of others and identify a scapegoat. That is easy enough to find. There is an almost unlimited amount of options in this area: parents, siblings, co-workers, spouses, bosses, friends, enemies and so on. How much closer does that get you to a solution for the problem?

"Running away from a problem only increases
the distance from the solution."
—Anonymous

Running away, blaming others, criticizing others or
something are not solutions. They are a manner in which
to momentarily escape your accountability in the issue.
They are not solutions, nor do they move you closer to
improving your life and the situation. True leaders will look
past these wastes of time and chose to lead in a healthy
manner. Choose to be a true leader of your life.

"If you can solve your problem, then what is the need
of worrying? If you cannot solve it, then what is the use of
worrying?"
—Shantideva, 8th-century Indian Buddhist scholar

The last option is to give up on attempting to solve
the problem. This will slowly lead to giving up on life. It is
one more step toward robbing your life of passions and joy.
Problems don't just suddenly go away, no matter how much
you want this to happen.

"Giving up is the most painful way of solving a problem."
—Anonymous

Think for a moment what you're communicating to
your spouse and/or co-workers when you give up. You're

staring them in the face and "saying" you're not worth it, the relationship is not worth it, that life is not worth it. How do you want to be seen by your loved ones? How do you want to be seen in the world? As an individual who solves problems, or wants others to solve it for them?

There are an unlimited number of problems in the world, and they don't stop one day. How do you want to meet the next problem in your life? Complaining? No one is listening. Blaming? It will come right back to you. Running? This doesn't solve or support anything positive in your life. What kind of person do you want to be in your world? Start now with that problem that has been staring you in the face for too long. Don't stop until it is solved.

How do you start to solve that problem? Allow for quiet time to dissect the issue. Confide in those you trust and ask for their feedback. Who would you ask? Take one small step to make progress. Read more about an individual who's faced a similar challenge. Action and progress are your greatest allies.

"No problem can withstand the assault of sustained thinking."
—VOLTAIRE, FRENCH WRITER

It is all within your mindset. As long as you see a problem as unsolvable, it is and will continue to be as such. You've not attempted every option, and so you must do something different until it works for you and your life.

"Bad times have scientific value. These are occasions a good learner would not miss."
—Ralph Waldo Emerson, American writer

The win comes when the problem is solved. You learn from the situation and you move forward with your life. It will give you strength and confidence to face a bigger problem and to support others to face theirs.

Bottom Line for Wisdom is the Beginning: I don't care for problems in my life, however they've arrived, and my only choice is to leave it there where it is, or move to action and work to remove it and change things so it's out of my life. Those are my options: leave it and let it grow, or work past it so that I become powerful enough to move beyond.

"The gem cannot be polished without friction, nor man perfected without trials."
—Chinese Proverb

Wisdom is the Beginning Personal Activity: What do you see as the top three problems in your life? What is the first small step you can take to solve or conquer each problem?

Change

Life's Challenge: Change is a dreaded word to many. It is uncomfortable because humans appreciate the known and the familiar. When change is coming, people wonder if life will be improved or leave us with less.

Those who've experienced difficulty or pain when change appeared will no doubt shy away from future change. It is not uncommon for people to use the past as an excuse to put off the future.

"CHANGE FROM ANY POINT OF VIEW IS NOT GOOD OR BAD.
IT IS SIMPLY AN UNCOMFORTABLE PART OF LIFE."

Some don't like, avoid, and fight against change, while others eat it up, look for it, thrive in it. This fact leads to the truth that one's view on change is a choice and can be influenced. If you find yourself believing change is uncomfortable, know that it is possible to move your position and that change is not good or bad; it is simply an outcome of past experience. Which state of mind will lead you to a more satisfied life? We often forget that the past is not always an accurate predictor of the future, and change is a fact of life. We must find a way to mentally embrace change and manage ourselves through the course.

"All things are only transitory."
—JOHANN WOLFGANG VON GOETHE, GERMAN POET

Wisdom is the Beginning: There is change up ahead in life. I guarantee it.

Logically, it makes sense that people who've had traumatic experiences will shy away from change. On the flip side, those who've experienced success during change will look forward to what life has to offer. No matter past experience, change is often difficult to start, rough in the middle, and life-changing in the end.

"Things do not change; we change."
—HENRY DAVID THOREAU, AMERICAN ESSAYIST

It is a fact that life is full of changes. It is, always has been, and always will be. No matter your feelings about change, it is here and will be here. You cannot influence what lies ahead. You have but one note to play—you can decide how you allow change into your life and the mental preparedness you create to deal with newness.

"Everyone thinks of changing the world, but no one things of changing himself."
—Leo Tolstoy, Russian novelist

For those of you who hope to leave a lasting influence on the world, the most impactful long- lasting way is to become mentally healthy and strong. Not only will this impact your life and assist in accomplishing your desires, but it also has the power to demonstrate to those around you how to achieve their goals and dreams, breeding more love and health in every interaction.

"The universe is change; our life is what our thoughts make it."
—Marcus Aurelius, Roman leader

When you choose to not seek and embrace change, you choose to stay stuck. You rob yourself of the power to influence the situation and manner in which change happens. Choose instead to act in your power and influence the change in your world. Decide for yourself how you will accept a situation and work in it to get through it. Your actions will be fruitful over time to do anything but nothing.

"Change your opinions, keep to your principles; change your leaves, keep intact your roots."
—Victor Hugo, French poet

Not changing might work in the short term. Over a lifetime, though, choosing not to change will end up with a smaller and tighter comfort zone. There will be little room left to feel the joys and passions of life. It could mean a more fitting career move or searching for a new opening that brings more joy and passion.

At age 33, I was diagnosed with cancer, and after I completed treatment and had recovered I avoided change and went back into my same professional position. Something was not right, I blamed the new boss, I didn't feel challenged, and I blamed those around me. It wasn't till I became honest with myself and thought about it deeply that I determined I needed a change in my professional life. The cancer had changed pieces of my views and motivations; I needed to embrace change instead of looking for the same.

"Loss is nothing else but change, and change is Nature's delight."
—MARCUS AURELIUS, ROMAN LEADER

Change is the ultimate proof that you're living! If you've not felt that uncomfortable sensation in the pit of your stomach in months or years, then it has been too long. You must become open and seek change in life to push the edges of success. Instead of waiting for it to come to you, you must go and find it. When you know you are more than capable to deal with the unknown, then you are in control of your life.

"Life belongs to the living, and he who lives must be prepared for changes."
—Johann Wolfgang von Goethe, German poet

Begin now to have the internal confidence and strength to know that you'll come out on the other side of change with new skills and strength. Know that your mental perception of change is the battleground, not what change creates externally.

"Change begins in the mind and happens from the inside out."

The biggest mistake an individual can make is expecting that if they wait long enough, the change they want to happen in their life/relationship/job or project will happen. The truth is the same thing that is currently happening will continue to happen until you make a conscious effort to influence the direction. Do something different, now!

"If you want something you have never had, you must be willing to do something you have never done."
—Thomas Jefferson, Founding Father, Third President of the U.S.A.

When you choose not to embrace change, what is your reality? Your reality is then shaped by nothingness or by frustration. The more rigid a person becomes in life, the greater the chance of breaking. Life will not stop; change is one of the most powerful forces in your life. You can move with it and influence it, or it has the potential to break your spirits.

"CHANGE IS UP TO YOU."

Change *is* up to you; however, deciding not to change is a painful and unwise choice. Think about who you admire in your life. Is it those who embrace change, and look for newness, or those who are rigid and seek more of the same?

"The most faithful mirror is an old friend."
—ATTICUS, ANCIENT GREEK PHILOSOPHER

Embrace change, look for it, and invite trusted friends to look back on how you've grown in the process, and where the next change would benefit you most. Seek out a mentor in your life who'll assist in finding your next opportunity and guide you.

Bottom Line for Wisdom is the Beginning: If there is something in your past that is keeping you from embracing change, search it out and heal that wound. By healing, bringing logic and fact to a past situation, you can equip yourself to learn that change is to be expected and embraced. By leaving the past where it is, it pollutes today and keeps you from the biggest life possible.

> "There is nothing permanent except change."
> —HERACLITUS, GREEK PHILOSOPHER

Wisdom is the Beginning Personal Activity: What is your past experience with change? Did it bring excitement or discomfort? In the moments where it was uncomfortable, what were the other empowering feelings? At the least, find some value in those difficult times.

Relationship

Life's Challenge: There is a short list of key memory-making events in life. A few might be: your first pay check, your first love, having a best friend, obtaining your driver's license and more. I suggest the majority of the most impactful and lifetime memories involve your most loved relationships in your life. Therefore, examining how to do your part to make them healthy and successful is a valued endeavor.

Like all things in nature, relationships grow or die. The key part of that equation is either they grow together or grow apart; that is the choice of those in relationship. You can have your dreams, your spouse can have their dreams, but it is vital to have relationship dreams and direction too. To foster growth in your surroundings, create a safe and trusting environment where dreams and passions can be discussed and encouraged.

You want the relationship, long for it, need that other person in your life and don't know what to do with them when you have them. There is no complete list of rules and guidelines for how each individual wants to be treated. Nor do you hand everyone (or anyone) you meet your list of values, life goals, ideas and passions.

Yet often you are surprised and/or hurt when relationships fail; there were feelings of being let down, when they don't receive what they wanted in the relationship (even though neither party ever verbally expressed the existence of deep dreams, passions, and desire for intimacy).

Wisdom is the Beginning: You must go to the basics of what makes a successful relationship; communicate with your loved ones as to what is important for you to receive and how you both want to be treated.

Here is the starting place of relationship. They are imperfect, life is unfair, marriages are difficult, there will be fights, you cannot read their mind, and you are at least half of the problem.

> "Weakness on both sides is, as we know,
> the motto of all quarrels."
> —Voltaire, French writer

I believe this Voltaire quote is incredibly wise. Many individuals believe they are coming from a place of strength when they "stand their ground" or "fight it out" with their spouse. I take the other side. Basically, all fights come from a place of feeling less assured and full of doubt in one's self or in the relationship. Couples often fight to "be right", "not be told what to do" or "prove a point." However, these all come from a place of lack or feeling unloved. Once you feel truly strong, then you can allow the other person to express their own thoughts and opinions within a quarrel. Acknowledge the other person's decision and engage in discussion on your point of view.

"JUST BECAUSE WE DISAGREE IN NO WAY DOES IT MEAN I'M REJECTING YOU."

Therein we find the quandary, how do individuals work to a place of truly feeling strong (or confident, or loved, or at peace)? Making peace with the past, healing your oldest wounds and practicing forgiveness (for others and yourself) are the most powerful positions to start. All these steps will lead to you loving the other person, and you must truly love yourself first.

"If you wish to be loved, love."
—HECATO, GREEK STOIC PHILOSOPHER

The unfortunate unbreakable law of love is that if you're unable to give it to yourself, no one is able to fill you up. You'll long for it, you'll receive it, but it is like a bucket with holes in the bottom. Love can be poured into the bucket by those in your life, but it flows right though. Only you can heal your past which will put a healthy bucket in place.

"Needy people are demanding people."

Do your healing work and fill your own bucket or the relationship will suffer over the long term.

Every morning you can wake up and you have the choice to view the relationship as the same-old, same-old as it has been for the past x number of years, or you can choose to see it as a new beginning together. You don't marry once; you marry every single morning you awake.

"The person you married 10, 15, 40 years ago is no longer here."

Another way to approach it is to make the choice to focus on the beautiful relationship memories. If you do not, your default choice will be focusing on their imperfections. It is your choice. Think and focus on day 1 of your relationship: what was most important, most inviting, most attractive?

All of these are an internal decision on your behalf. Your relationships will go where you focus your thoughts. Do you focus on the last disagreement, or on the loving actions since you met that person?

"Marriage is three parts love and seven parts forgiveness of sins."
—Laozi, Chinese philosopher

The single most important act in a relationship, above

all, is to keep your agreements! Keep your spoken and unspoken agreements in your relationship. Those bonds are strengthened or destroyed one agreement at a time. This is the number one way to build safety and trust into your home.

What is key for your relationship? Love. What is important for love? Trust. What is essential for trust? Openness. What is necessary for openness? Words. What is key for words? Conversation. Keep and nurture your conversations. They will lead to love. If you talk only about the weather every day of your relationship, there will be no relationship in the end.

"YOUR LOVED ONES CAN DO NOTHING WITH NOTHING."

You must keep talking about things that matter. When you choose to shut down verbally and emotionally, the relationship is slowly and painfully murdered. Both adults (and the children) lose big.

You'll love and be loved. One day you'll understand that **to love** is the answer. Loving effort is attractive.

In the following chapters, you will take a look at differing area of relationships in more detail:

- I Can Change Him/Her
- My Partner Should Agree with Me
- Everyone Should Like Me
- People Will let You Down
- Addictions

Relationship: I Can Change Him/Her

Life's Challenge: Relationships come into your life like that of a seemingly perfect flower. So pure, so sweet, so exact; then you notice the first flaw. If you could just change the one flaw, all would be back in place perfectly. Then you "pluck" that imperfect petal. Oh, now the flower is out of balance. Just pluck a few more petals from the other side and... Now a mess has been made and everything that was once right is wrong.

This is how it begins, when we believe we can make one (or two or three or more) small changes to them: if they'd just be more like me, all would be wonderful. Then it goes all wrong and they will not change.

Typically, this realization takes place about 6 to 7 years into the relationship, after both are fully committed.

The time line looks something like this:	
Year 1 to 2	Awesome with raging hormones
Years 3 to 6	Work to change your partner
Year 7 (itch)	Begin to understand you cannot change them

Wisdom is the Beginning:

"YOU DON'T HAVE TO AGREE WITH THEM, BUT YOU DO
HAVE TO LIVE WITH THEM."

We are all imperfect. We are all unfinished.
Relationship and love are powerful forces in our lives.
Once attraction is set, nothing else matters for the two
involved in the dance. All we can see, in the beginning,
are the perfect perfections. We absolutely ignore the flaws,
damage and unhealthy habits. No matter what our closest
confidant, mentor, or parent might say, love conquers all,
for the moment.

"We are all full of weakness and errors; let us mutually pardon
each other our follies—it is the first law of nature."
—VOLTAIRE, FRENCH WRITER

Too often you are attracted to an opposite or different
personality type from your own. It completes you on some
level. Then your respect for their gifts and strengths slips

into annoyance and you just want them to change a bit. You start to wonder and believe that if they were just a little more like you, this relationship would be much more successful.

At some point you've lost sight of the differences that attracted you in the first place and that being in relationship with someone "just like me" would have bored you to tears.

> "It is not the lack of love, but a lack of friendship, that makes unhappy marriages."
> —FRIEDRICH NIETZSCHE, GERMAN PHILOSOPHER

Do you treat your friends and judge them as harshly as you judge your closest relationship? You accept differences in your friends but can't stand them in your partners. What you are saying is, if brutally honest, you are right and they are wrong; your way is better and you know what is best.

This poses the question: Would you rather be right or happy? By fighting about every differing decision or personal choice, how happy does that make you and the relationship? (Additionally, how do those who are around you appreciate it?)

> "YOU CANNOT GET THE TIME BACK YOU WASTED FUSSING AND FIGHTING."

Do you have the ability to respect their strengths and love their weaknesses? If you do not, then each passing year you will become more entrenched in your beliefs. The set-up of "I'm right" and they are "wrong" is a never-ending stand-off, and the foundation of the relationship is starved. How long would you stick to a relationship where you were always wrong? How much would you invest to make it better?

"You can only change you."

Any and all change is up to the individual 100 percent. As long as you're expecting the other person to act a certain way, you'll be disappointed. Change you and work for a safe and trusting environment, and the best will happen in the relationship. Before you spend any more energy attempting to change that other person, look at what you can and need to change within yourself first.

"In order for others to feel safe, you must create a safe environment."

We all have imperfections; why is it that we cannot accept that fact in others? We've all done things that have hurt others, we've said things to our loved ones that we regret, we expect change but don't want to change. Imperfections are all around us and in us.

"YOU CAN LOVE THROUGH IMPERFECTIONS."

Create space for individuality in your relationship, and let the other live their own life. Support and acceptance for the other individual will bring you peace and permission to do the same in your life. It is a blessing and will only bring you more of what you want in your life. Release; they must live with their decisions.

Bottom Line for Wisdom is the Beginning: Stop expecting people to be the way you want them to be; everything starts with yourself.

Relationship: My Partner Should Agree with Me

Life's Challenge: Somewhere along the way, the Fairytale vs. Reality of relationship became intertwined to the point that it causes huge issues in your love today. The most damaging intersection of this intertwinement is at the point of "to be deeply in love we must agree on every important topic." This sets up the situation that when my other half of the relationship doesn't agree with me, then they are rejecting me as a person.

Wisdom is the Beginning: Consider your goal of the last important conversation or disagreement that you experienced. If the result is for both parties to have a mutual point of understanding, then that is a healthy outcome and goal. That also means you'll have to give and respect other's points of view, and they will have to respect yours.

"DISAGREEMENT DOES NOT EQUAL REJECTION."

If the goal is simply for the other party to agree with your point of view, you're building something that won't hold. The result of the agreement must create a situation where both parties feel they've been heard and supported on the path to obtain what is important to them.

> "Victor and vanquished never unite in substantial agreement."
> —TACITUS, ROMAN HISTORIAN

What is the goal of the relationship? To be the victor or to move forward in agreement?

If you always win and they lose, how long will they invest in the relationship to make it better?

There's always this one fight, argument, disagreement that you've had 500 times in your relationship. You know it so well that you know what the other person is going to say. No doubt you will find yourself in a similar conversation in the near future. What are the options in this situation? The key is to do something different, to stop repeating the same fight with the same outcome. With no common ground, you are destined to face the issue again. Until you actively do something different and search for the healthy solution, peace will not be found.

> "A bad peace is worse than war."
> —TACITUS, ROMAN HISTORIAN

I do believe that conflict in relationship is a natural

state and can be healthy. Personally, more worrying to me is when there is no conflict at all—silence is deadly. However, the type of conflict experienced is vital, whether it is healthy conflict. Once a relationship starts to go deeper and the topics become more important—idea, thoughts, opinions, dreams—then people will disagree. The use of silence will kill off all opportunity for deeper conversation and understanding.

Let me share this realization with you. There is a tiny shift in viewpoint that will pay huge dividends in your relationship. It is not about agreement, rather it is about both parties leaving with what they want. Finding this place will move the relationship into more love, peace and success. It is not about agreement, but is about creating a successful fulfilling relationship for both individuals.

Make no mistake that "silence" is a key form of communication. Saying nothing is an option sometimes, but not all the time. There is such a thing as a healthy silence. There is also an act of unhealthy silence known as shutting down (also known as unhealthy conflict). Unhealthy silence says one of a few things: 1) this relationship is dead, or 2) I don't care enough to participate, or 3) I'm emotionally dead. Love equals the fact that, after a disagreement or a period of silence, there is still love. A deep relationship without disagreement doesn't exist.

"The ear is the avenue to the heart."
—VOLTAIRE, FRENCH WRITER

While disagreement and conflict will enter and be a part of relationships, how you choose to conduct yourself during the conversation has huge bearing on the potential success for the situation. Will you act in a way that establishes long term trust and safety? Will you build on a foundation and keep your agreements on how to speak to a loved one? Will you keep to the "rules of engagement" that you've established with your partner? What are you communicating with your body language (closed, eye rolling, exhaling loudly)?

"We often refuse to accept an idea merely because the tone of voice in which it has been expressed is unsympathetic to us."
—FRIEDRICH NIETZSCHE, GERMAN PHILOSOPHER

It has been proven in many situations that our messages (our conversations) are communicated in many forms beyond words. There are numerous factors: tone, volume, body language, facial features, vocabulary, inflection. Over and over, studies have shown that only 7 percent of messages are communicated in your words and 93 percent communicated with other aspects of your voice and body.

Please, when you have an important conversation, don't do it over text message. The other person is only receiving 7 percent of the message.

"We cannot wish for that we know not."
—VOLTAIRE, FRENCH WRITER

Do you control your temper, tone, and body language in your important conversations? Give the gift to yourself and your relationship, and communicate your message in a 100 percent respectful manner.

Understand that disagreement doesn't necessarily lead to rejection in your communication; however if one individual does believe they are (constantly) rejected, then a hostile war-like environment is created. How is this so, and where does this lead the relationship over time? If disagreement does end in rejection in the mind of the participant, then a winner or a loser situation is established and the relationships cannot flourish. If you create a war environment, a win/lose situation, then all lose. A relationship cannot grow and flourish when one half of it loses.

"WHAT ARE YOU REALLY FIGHTING ABOUT IN YOUR RELATIONSHIP?"

Take the time and effort to look back on your life and examine your past pains. All too often what you are fighting about it is a wound from your past that has not been fully healed and is creeping into your life today. The walls you build will not serve you in relationship. They will keep out most hurts and all joys. You cannot cut off one area of feeling; it is all or nothing.

Discovering what you're really hurt about, what still pains you from your past, will bring clarity to the way you're reacting to a seemingly small issue today. Without allowing any space for disagreements, you and your partner leave many important things unsaid. Shift your position just a little. Consider the goal to be 100 percent vulnerability and allow the other to see and know all there is to know about you; in return, accept their growing vulnerability.

Bottom Line for Wisdom is the Beginning: The healthiest starting point is to create an environment where both partners can express their deepest ideas, dreams, wants, and so on. Then both partners work to support their dreams and the dreams of the other half. As my partner achieves her dreams, she become more alive in life and, in turn, supports my dreams with passion. That is the type of partner I want in my house!

"THOSE WHO BELIEVE THAT ABSOLUTE AGREEMENT
EQUALS TRUE LOVE HAS NEVER BEEN,
AND NEVER WILL BE, IN LOVE."

Relationship: Everyone Should Like Me

Life's Challenge: There is a certain sub-set of the population that is not concerned in the least with other's opinion of them and their personality. However, most of us want to be liked and some of us think everyone should or will like us all the time. We must be conscious of what the desire to be liked costs us within ourselves and those around us whom we love.

Wisdom is the Beginning:

> "Love is no assignment of cowards."
> —OVID, ROMAN POET

Being liked by people around you is important. As social creatures, and from an evolutionary point of view, it is vital to human survival to be part of the group. If you were not liked by the group and kicked out, then your chances of survival would be at risk.

More and more studies are being published about how important relationships are to you in life. Those who have close social groups live healthier and longer. There are big rewards to being liked and loved. However, this mindset can be taken too far and be unhealthy. As you've seen in previous chapters, conflict is part of any relationship that ventures beyond small talk. How you internalize not being liked, and feel about it, is the vital mental view.

Everyone wants to be liked especially by loved ones, however, what are you giving up in exchange for being liked?

The Action/Decision to be "Liked"	Result
Break agreements and overcommit (to be liked)	Broken trust
White lies (to be liked)	No respect
Focusing on unimportant interaction	Not being present for key relationships

You have a tool within your power to greatly impact the quality of your relationships. Thankfully it has very little gray area and is clear cut. That tool is keeping (breaking) agreements and acting/living as a trustworthy partner. It builds and strengthens the base of relationship, therefore No base = No love.

The lesson is to only make agreements you can keep and speak your truth. This might mean that you're not always liked in the moment or by the individual. However, the bigger question is: What is more important in life than being liked? It is Respect, Love and Trust.

"LIFE IS NOT ABOUT BEING LIKED; IT IS ABOUT BEING LOVED AND RESPECTED."

Love also means saying "No" especially to others outside of the relationship. Love sometimes means butting head with bosses, authority, and extended family. You'll not always be liked, but you can be loved and/or respected.

The **need** to be nice and liked above all else is often about lack of self-esteem and having no confidence. You seek others to validate what you won't give to yourself or can internally accept. If you like yourself, does it really matter what the rude person thinks of you?

"If we have not peace within ourselves,
it is in vain to seek it from outward sources."
—FRANCOIS DE LA ROCHEFOUCAULD,
FRENCH WRITER AND MEMOIRIST

Bottom Line for Wisdom is the Beginning: There are as many reasons we seek life partners, as many reasons as there are individuals. However, there is one truth that slowly escapes as the years pass; we want them to grow closer to us, and our lives to grow together, for them to obtain their dreams in life. When we focus on the foundational part of our relationship, it will become more fulfilling, loving, and supportive.

Relationship: People Will Let You Down

Life's Challenge: We tie our life so closely to others that it will inevitably cause us issue in our own lives.

We love someone so much, we have impactful and positive experiences with them, and they do and say things that are beyond our initial expectations, so we raise their status in our minds. Then, they meet and exceed those too. At some point we've built up such a grand idea of this person that at some point they fall short—way too short.

"WHEN YOU ARE ATTACHED TO THE OUTCOME OF OTHER'S ACTIONS, YOU WILL BE DISAPPOINTED."

Wisdom is the Beginning: What is at the root of feeling let down by another individual? Your own judgments? Judgments are a fact of life; you have them in most situations and individuals you encounter. They pollute your interactions and experience of the world if you never stop to check out if they are true and valid.

> "We are all strong enough to bear other men's misfortunes."
> —Francois de la Rochefoucauld, French writer and memoirist

Your judgments of your partners (or significant other) continually get in your way about how you interact and react to their decisions on how they live their lives. The bottom line is that their actions and decisions are their business. When you met them and started a friendship or dated, their actions (to a degree) were your concern, so this is the time to understand them and see if you aligned in a significant manner. Once the trial phase has passed and now that you've fully committed to them, how are you spending your energy, focused on each and every action of theirs? As long as you're caught up in "they should do this or that," then they will let you down. Don't spend your relationship thinking and feeling perturbed about: how someone washes dishes, how much they leave the bedroom window open, how they drive across town.

Acknowledge there are different ideas and manners to accomplish a goal and focus on big wins for both lives.

Consider the ultimate goal for your relationship. Is it acceptance (of others and self), peace, harmony, mutual support? And when ideals don't perfectly align, work to an agreement or allow the tension to release.

Do you expect perfection from those around you? Take a step back and consider that it is impossible to meet the standard of perfection. What happens is that you create distance in relationships when the bar is set too high. You'll connect with others through your weakness and vulnerabilities. If all I see is strength and perfection in you, then I cannot relate as I'm not perfect. I can relate to the challenges you've faced and your imperfections. This is the space where individuals come together and bond, when vulnerability is allowed and encouraged.

"GET OUT OF YOUR JUDGMENTS AND LIVE LIFE."

A truth about relationships is that the things you love and respect will let you down when you get close. Perception and reality are not the same.

You will be hurt in life, and people will let you down. As we've seen in this chapter, it is all about how you handle, or choose not to handle, these facts of life. If you allow these circumstances to take over, they will turn you into a bitter and resentful person.

Will you continue to live in your judgments of what should be, or move to a place of acceptance of what simply is? Will you allow someone else's opinion to count more than yours? At some point, if you give away your power and allow it, someone else will gladly run your life with their opinions. Many people would love to take on that task, however, you'll never again be priority #1.

When someone lets you down, is it about you or them? When you are brutally honest with yourself, all too often you believe that it is about you and your poor judgments/expectations that got you into trouble again. You take another's actions and decisions onto yourself. It doesn't work for you. Does someone else's poor decisions mean your decisions are less successful or valid? No, disconnect yourself from other's actions and decisions. Bottom line, you're only responsible for your own.

Here's something else I've learned:

> "ONLY JUDGE YOURSELF VERSUS YOURSELF
> AS YOU WERE YESTERDAY."

Work to become a little more powerful every single day. Become powerful enough to know not every decision is going to be correct and that you have the ability to pick yourself up and continue to be the most perfect person to run your life.

Bottom Line for Wisdom is the Beginning: Others are imperfect; understand and forgive, or forgive and release. Only you can determine if you are lovable because no one else has that power.

Relationship: Addictions

Life's Challenge: One of life's biggest challenges for the individual and the family/friends is when addictions are an issue in life. Those struggling with addictions have lost complete control of the situation and their life, and I mean complete control. It is a struggle for all who are involved and touched by the addict and the addiction.

In addition to addictions such as alcohol, tobacco, street drugs and prescription drugs, it will serve us all well to take an honest look at our unhealthy habits. While these habits may not be as overtly damaging and deadly as those listed above, they are especially harmful to us over time. We can improve our lives greatly by becoming internally honest and looking at those habits, stopping them and replacing them with a habit that is healthy.

Some of the habits that are severely damaging to ourselves and families are: eating too much refined sugar, foods heavy with salt, and a high fat diet. Others are spending too much time on the sofa watching mindless television, or spending too much time gaming; also consider overuse of electronic gadgets and social media overload.

Without internal honesty, the habit or addiction will continue and slowly, then quickly, eat away at your time and quality of life. Choosing to ignore the situation and hope for change will lead to a less healthy life.

Wisdom is the Beginning: The definition of addiction from the Center on Addiction is more complete: Addiction is a complex disease, often chronic in nature, which affects the functioning of the brain and body. It also causes serious damage to families, relationships, schools, workplaces and neighborhoods. The most common symptoms of addiction are severe loss of control, continued use despite serious consequences, preoccupation with using the substance, failed attempts to quit, tolerance and withdrawal. Addictions incur great cost in our lives, to our loved ones, our families and society. It costs precious years and lives.

If you and your family face addiction, how you deal with the addiction is the key issue. While concealing it in the beginning might be the usual pattern, it is not a solution. Addictions cannot be concealed to reach a healthy state. It is not only the addict who is sick; the unfortunate truth is the family is just as affected.

"THE SECRET IS THERE ARE NO SECRETS."

Keeping secrets locked up inside is not a solution. I

believe that secrets make us sick. The addiction does not mean you and the family are not loving or caring; it means they have a problem in life and use a chemical, act, or outside source to escape.

"We do not despise all those who have vices, but we do despise those that have no virtue."
—Francois de la Rochefoucauld, French writer and memoirist

Addictions are unfortunate, sad, and cost society a great deal in health care, families breaking up and general dysfunction. However, individuals in addiction are not in control of their life. They and those in relationship must get help, there are numerous programs available, and the most important step is to find one that benefits you and your family. That is a true winner, a person of virtue to one who seeks assistance.

Let's make this very clear:

"Chemicals are not your friend."

I must pose an uneasy question to all readers. What is your addiction? If it is too difficult to digest in those words, what is your unhealthy habit? We all have one, whether it is food we eat in excess, too much gaming, and so on.

The most socially acceptable form of addiction is work.

"I found the perfect addiction -workaholic-
it is so socially acceptable."
—Unknown

What is your favorite escape route? It doesn't work for you. Deal with it now and remove it from your life. Immediately replace it with a healthy act or substance. If you cannot deal with it by yourself, find help now.

"Addictions don't make you happy; they just mask what makes you sad."

Then, or in conjunction with changing habits, after you start to become healthy, forgiveness is needed. It works in the healing (where needed and appropriate) of yourself and others. Only at this point, with the addiction under control and forgiveness started, can the individual focus on improving the key relationships in their life.

"Forgiveness is a decision; it may need to be made more than once."

Forgiveness is the greatest gift you can give yourself and others. It doesn't mean what happened or what they did was right, however, holding onto unforgiveness only creates bitterness.

"Holding on to anger is like grasping a hot coal with the intent of throwing it at someone else; you are the one who gets burned."
—BUDDHA, PHILOSOPHER

It is a gift for you to work on forgiveness. The flip side is ugly. Bitterness is the curse of not forgiving. It poisons your relationships and your life.

Bottom Line for Wisdom is the Beginning: Love yourself, love those in your life struggling with addictions and accept outside help.

Rejection

Life's Challenge: Oh, rejection—one of the most unpleasant parts of life. Everyone knows it is coming, but there is no way to lessen the sting. We'll face rejection professionally, personally, in our volunteer positions, with our children, with our pets. It is all around us; it ebbs and flows.

Rejection is part of life, something that we cannot control. What we can control is how we allow rejection to impact us after we experience it, and how we allow it to influence us moving forward.

Wisdom is the Beginning:

> "There is nothing good or bad, but thinking makes it so."
> —SHAKESPEARE, PLAYWRIGHT

The slightest change in your thoughts and your beliefs about rejections will have an incredible impact on your life. You must leave behind the thought that rejection is "bad" as the Shakespeare quote suggests. When you choose to change "rejection = bad" to "rejection = information," then your success over a lifetime will compound greatly. Think about what would happen to a person who internalized and believed that every piece of rejection was accurate. They would be carrying around an incredible weight, and it would only grow in size over time. By choosing to see that the rejection received as information to redirect their path, closer to their goal, they can use it to their benefit.

Take it one step further; rejection can change your life in a positive direction. Rejection can be positive, and in the moment, it is simply too soon to tell what is the new ending point. It might be that the "No" you've received is temporary, and that at a future point will change to acceptance.

"SEE REJECTION AS A START OF NEW POSSIBILITIES."

With relationships, it is easy to see that while it is often labeled as rejection, it is no more than life's way to redirect, to move you to the next phase. Would you really want to be with someone who was not committed to giving their best? Embrace the rejection and look for the next opportunity.

The biggest issue about continuing to see the rejection as a painful point is that the next episode of rejection is just around the corner. When it is about to arrive, then what type of mindset will you have? If you see rejection as a "slap in the face," then you're in trouble. Slaps hurt, shut you down, and make you hesitant. Rejection is nothing more than redirection. When you make it more than that, you give too much power to other individuals to have input into your life. Rejection is meaningless in your life, unless you choose to see it as others giving information to improve. That is something that is beneficial.

When information is received in the form of rejection, you can approach it in the following manners:

- Dismiss the information (that is, Rejection) completely and outright. This gives up any opportunity for growth (Redirection). A complete and outright wasted opportunity.
- Internalize the information and examine it for the opportunity to grow. If there is valid information, then you can grow from it (i.e., Redirect your life). Maybe there is newer or more accurate information, and so you disregard the rejection and move on.
- Bonus if you continue to receive the same information (Rejection) from outside sources, it is time to look at it honestly to see what you're doing to give this impression.

Is rejection the end of the book or simply the start of the next chapter? The good news is that it is your choice. Information is power. It gives you the opportunity to grow, leads to more in life, success, and it means people care. If people don't give you information, they don't care enough about you or the situation. If they care enough to give you information, then they care about your outcome.

Rejection is painful for a few hours or days. Regret last years or worse, your final thought. Death is not the worst-case scenario, but never living and improving on your life is the saddest outcome of all.

When you're doing amazing things with your life, you'll face a load of rejection. Not only are you doing new things, but you're also changing people's perception of reality.

We've examined "rejection" going only one direction—heading towards you. Now let's look at it from the other point of view—coming from you. Do you reject others too easily? Do you reject instead of giving insightful information? It is easy to outrightly reject. It is enlightening to lend a hand. Whatever you want in your life, be sure you're giving it too.

"REJECTION SAYS MORE ABOUT THEM THAN ME."

Bottom Line for Wisdom is the Beginning: Learning to take "rejection" as a form of information to help you grow will make a lifetime of difference. This mindset will allow you to receive differing viewpoints and use the information to take you to new heights and directions. What if the information they're giving you is accurate? What if you can grow, based on the information? Once you've determined your answers, put the information to use and discard what is not of value to you.

> "Our greatest glory is not in never falling,
> but rising every time we fall."
> —CONFUCIUS, CHINESE PHILOSOPHER

Wisdom is the Beginning Personal Activity: Where do you feel rejection in your life as you examine your past? What is the truth today? Was it rejection or simply a redirection? Was it rejection, or not right now? In the moment, it often feels like rejection, but looking back with clarity can bring newness. Until we re-examine past events, we are stuck with our original experience and decisions. Do you reject often? Do you reject easily?

Self-Limiting

Life's Challenge: Self-Limiting means to restrict (knowledge gain, or emotional) growth by your own actions. It includes believing you have no control over what happens and how you react to the challenges of life, or in blaming others for everything that happens in your life. It may also involve engaging in wishful or small thinking about a situation, not using your gifts or passions and remaining speechless.

Can you fill in the blanks for the following questions?
The harshest judges of my life are...
The biggest critics I will face are...
The individual who holds me back most in my life is...
The person who speaks most harshly to me is...
The person who limits me the most in life is...
The person I play the most self-defeating games with is...
The biggest dream killer in my life is...
The individual most likely to rob me of my passion is...

The person who is most likely to blame for poor relationships is...
What single answer came up most for you? Was it: Me?

When you learn to get out of your own way, life becomes more peaceful. Many aspects of life are challenging and difficult. There are very few quick wins of substance, and for many there are none. You must provide the internal engine focus to obtain your goals in life. Once you learn to curb aspects of self-limiting behaviors, then success is assured. What you think and believe about your life will come true; it can go either way, for or against you.

"There is nothing in the world more shameful than establishing one's self on lies and fables."
—JOHANN WOLFGANG VON GOETHE, GERMAN POET

Wisdom is the Beginning: The lie which most limits, confines, restricts and controls lives is: "That's just the way I am." A close relative of this is: "I was born this way." When you believe that there is nothing better, no growth possible, no chance for more joy or passion in life nor improvement in your relationships, then you are stuck exactly where you are. To believe that there is more to life is to know that you are not done living.

"The greater part of our happiness or misery depends upon our dispositions, and not upon our circumstance."
—Martha Washington, wife of George Washington, First President of the United States

Excuses, excuses—they do nothing for you. Completely remove them from your life and wording. Be aware of where you lay blame, for doing so comes out in your behavior. Even if you're not 100 percent responsible for the situation, take control of your part. By blaming and living in that space, you're only weakening yourself and showing those around you that you're not one to be followed.

"I attribute my success to this: I never gave or took any excuse."
—Florence Nightingale, pioneer of modern nursing

You are (possibly) horribly limiting your own life unknowingly. There are no limits on what career you can pursue. Whatever kind of home life you create, or your level of self-esteem, accept the limits you place on yourself—what you think or decide you deserve. To some extent you cannot control what happens in your life, but you have all the control of how it impacts your life.

"It is man's own mind, not his enemy or foe, that lures him to evil ways."
—Buddha, philosopher

When difficulties enter your life, know that you have a choice to take control of your thoughts and decide your best action forward. All begins with your thoughts. There can be no action before thought. There can be no leadership before thought. There can be no passionate future without thought.

"If one speaks or acts with a pure mind, happiness follows him like a shadow that never leaves him"
—BUDDHA SCRIPTS, DHAMMAPADA VERSE 2

The comfort zones you build for yourself are the biggest killer of your own greatness. Living the fullest life possible is up to you. Don't wait for the princess or prince to come into your life to take you to greatness; that's part of a past narrative. Start to be what you want to become right now. Life doesn't become more by chance; it's only when you embrace change that it happens.

"He who does not think much of himself is much more esteemed than he imagines."
—JOHANN WOLFGANG VON GOETHE, GERMAN POET

Finally, choose to be involved in your own life. Make your decisions your priority. If you give your life to someone else, they will run and ruin it for you. If you choose the latter; believe me you won't like where it goes.

How would believing in yourself 100 percent make your life different?

In the upcoming chapters, we'll look at some of the most self-limiting acts:

- No Time
- I'm Tired
- Not Enough X
- Life out of Balance
- Waiting for Life to Happen
- Guilt

Self-Limiting: No Time

Life's Challenge: You must choose to control the limited resources you have. If you don't, they will control you. Time is something everyone deals with and is of a limited supply. If you are not aware, then you stop running your schedules, and time runs you. Therefore, when time is running you, it will lead to broken agreements, lost trust, stress and poor relationships.

> "One always has time enough, if one will apply it well."
> —JOHANN WOLFGANG VON GOETHE, GERMAN POET

No doubt there are an incredible number of commitments pulling on your lives today. You can be as busy as you want to be. To add to the stress, the addition of the cell phone and instant media distractions means your free time has gone to zero. You allow it to distract from what really matters in life and replace it with busy.

"The opposite of success isn't failure,
it is an excuse."

Wisdom is the Beginning: As discussed earlier, failure can be seen as a stepping stone to success. Excuses about "no time" are only used to make yourself feel temporarily better. They have no positive impact on the situation or relationship. In the situation, the damage is done, and so make the choice to move to accountability.

"Procrastination is the thief of time. Collar him!"
—Charles Dickens, English writer

Excuses will slowly end your life. Choose to remove excuses because they only limit you and your relationships. Choosing to make life happen and deal with what comes your way is pure personal accountability and a powerful manner to live life. When you are personally accountable for your life and what comes your way, you are completely responsible for your actions and decisions.

"He that is good for making excuses is seldom good for anything else."
—Benjamin Franklin, founding father of US
Declaration of Independence

Perhaps you're making excuses about not having time to spend with loved ones. By making yourself too busy, having no time, what are you communicating to those closest to you? That they don't fully matter, that you don't respect them? Be aware what you're costing yourself and your relationships by misplacing your priorities.

> "An excuse is worse and more terrible than a lie;
> for an excuse is a lie guarded."
> —ALEXANDER POPE, ENGLISH POET

Some might say that if there was more time in the day, then they could get everything done. However, there is no time management book that teaches how to add time to the day. This is about taking an honest look at your life and owning what you cost yourself in areas that really matter by saying "I have no time."

> "WE ALREADY HAVE ALL THE TIME THERE IS—USE
> IT WISELY."

As you remove excuses from life and become accountable for your decisions, one benefit will be increased focus on what is important, then prioritization of those areas becomes clear. When you choose not to prioritize, then all items fall off the list and the most important things in your life soon feel like they don't matter. Your careers, your children, and your relationships suffer because you allow unimportant commitments to enter.

Take time to dissect your life and understand which areas are "bloated" and which are "starved" for your time. It seems, all too often, that the family is where we take time from first and starve the longest.

> "Our life is frittered away by detail. Simplify, simplify."
> —HENRY DAVID THOREAU, AMERICAN ESSAYIST

Important versus unimportant, those two can be confusing. What are your top five priorities in life? Narrow it down to three. I'm sure you have your family and loved ones there. Does the manner in which you spend your time match up with how you view your top priorities? If it does not, then you're allowing unimportant commitments to lead you.

> "DON'T LET TIME GET IN THE WAY OF YOUR RELATIONSHIPS WITH PEOPLE."

What are you losing out on by filling your schedule with busy work? Find your passions in life and follow them with a full heart. Find your career passion and focus on it while keeping your relationships in balance. Busy work can quickly rob you of both.

> "Hardly any human being is capable of pursuing two professions or two arts rightly."
> —PLATO, GREEK PHILOSOPHER

Being "so busy" is a choice. You cost yourself your life by allowing unimportant things to enter. Clarity is a key to keeping balance, therefore focus on what is important for you, understand you have the right and duty to say "no" when life is slipping out of balance. When you're clear on how to divide your time that best suits you, the ride will be less bumpy.

> "Be happy for this moment. This moment is your life."
> —OMAR KHAYYAM, PERSIAN MATHEMATICIAN

Bottom Line for Wisdom is the Beginning: Clear out excuses and replace them with your truth and accountability. Your life, your stress, your peace of mind and your relationships will thank you for it.

> "Any excuse will serve a tyrant."
> —AESOP, GREEK FABULIST

Self-Limiting: I'm Tired

Life's Challenge: "How are you doing?" That's a typical question we receive every day. The typical answer has gone from "I'm well; how are you?" to "I'm so tired."

> "Life is one long process of getting tired."
> —SAMUEL BUTLER, THE YOUNGER, NOVELIST, SATIRIST, SCHOLAR

We've reached a point where we have so many distractions in our society that we exhaust ourselves on a daily basis, and it has become a societal norm that we must be busy and tired all the time. Life can turn into something like the hamster on the wheel running its heart out: get up, check your phone, get ready and eat as fast as possible, check your phone, commute to work, check your phone, work work work, commute home, sit on the sofa (either not long enough or way too long), watch reality tv, go to bed on the phone, and then start it all over again. This is exhausting and can go on for a year, decade or a lifetime.

Wisdom is the Beginning: Another self-limiting excuse people use more and more today is: "I'm Tired." It can be due to any number of reasons, many self-induced. Some may take on too much, day after day, and leave themselves "out of gas." Some may do too little, which often leads to doing less and feeling drained and tired. When it is a self-limiting tired, then the individual created it.

> "Life is too short, and the time we waste in yawning never can be regained."
> —STENDHAL, FRENCH AUTHOR, PROFESSOR

If you choose to idealize those around you who don't have a minute on their schedule, then you'll imitate them and fill your schedule too. If you want to have more (house, car, fashion, etc.) then you do what it takes to obtain those things. Will those items be on the top of your list 5 years from now? 10 years? 20 years?

The saddest life is one filled with nothing that matters. If you believe people around you expect you to be busy, then you'll live up to that expectation. The problem is that you lose what you most value. Which poses the question, what do you value most? What are your big lifetime dreams? What do you want more of in your life? Fill it with what matters most to you, or days will pass and be filled with memories that don't matter.

"Life is largely a matter of expectation."
—HORACE, AUTHOR (VERSION OF HOMER TEACHING)

There are times when "I'm tired" is true and real.
What to do with the sensation is key. Take care of yourself,
understand the reason you feel this way, move to a
healthier position in your life.

For me, when my body is tired, I rest, eat well and
soon it is ready to go. When my mind is tired, I ignore it,
change the activity and take a few minutes to relax.

"Either do not attempt at all, or go through with it."
—OVID, ROMAN POET

You must remove the excuse of "I'm tired" from your
vocabulary when it is just that—an excuse or throw-away
phrase—or is not accurate. You've made yourself tired, what
you say and think your body believes. It is a self-fulfilling
state of mind and body. It is no-one's doing except your
own. What is your pay-off for allowing yourself to be
in this external state? What is the benefit for yourself
and your life? Stop blaming others for this state, and do
something that focuses on what is important to you.

Bottom Line for Wisdom is the Beginning: Are you tired
because your mind is saying your body it is tired, or because
your body really is tired? One state is easy to remedy, the
other one is never ending. Utilized as an excuse, it robs you
and your loved ones.

Wisdom is the Beginning Personal Activity: What do you value most in your life that is not getting the attention it deserves because of the self-limiting behavior of "I'm tired?"

Self-Limiting: Not Enough X

Life's Challenge: Life is about limited resources. We can struggle all we want with this idea, however, it is a fact. There is never enough of everything for everyone. Our view on our resources is what we can control and experience as having enough. The feeling of contentment and having enough is right there. Will you choose to see it?

Wisdom is the Beginning: Right now, lack versus abundance is alive in you, alive in us all. It is not about what you do or do not have, rather it is about what you experience in your life. You've created this life; you've created lack or abundance. Now rejoice with what you've created and know that if you want to shift the scale, then you have the fortitude and will to make it so.

"A useless life is an early death."
—JOHANN WOLFGANG VON GOETHE, GERMAN POET

I've personally felt this way many times in my life. I don't have enough funds. I want a new career. I deserve closer friendships. When I catch myself in this frame of mind, I tack a "now" on the end. I don't have enough funds, right now. I want a new career, for now. I deserve closer friendships, right now. This clears where I'm spending my mental energies at the moment and where I want to examine my life to make changes. I give myself permission to want more x. More importantly, when I feel this way, I mentally examine it and make changes so I obtain what I want more of in my life. To feel it and not take action does little for my life.

"Be content with what you have; rejoice in the way things are. When you realize there is nothing lacking, the whole world belongs to you."
—Lao Tzu, Chinese philosopher

What will you choose to see in your life and relationships? Don't self-limit and choose to see lack. Some areas of your life are full and overflowing with gifts and joy, while other areas may experience scarcity and shortage. Create a life in which you can practice abundance. The view-point of lack is a choice; you will continue to experience it as such until you make a different choice. What are you looking for in your life?

"Man is made by his belief. As he believes, so he is."
—Bhagavad Gita, Hindu scripture

Go forth, make more, do more, be more, want more in your life. Do so for the experience in life, that you deserve to have those dreams. Action is your friend, find your next best small step in your situation. It seems simple, but one step leads to another which leads to new information, clarity and more action. You can lead yourself to a joyous life.

> "We forge the chains we wear in life."
> —CHARLES DICKENS, ENGLISH WRITER

There was a time in my life when I didn't believe it was within me to create what I desired. I can see that it was a lie that was keeping me stuck. I have relationships all around me, riches all around me, and health all around me too. We all have the inherent ability to create what we desire in life, which is abundance. Is it a matter of wanting more, or do I need to take inventory of what I do have and be at ease?

> "Reflect upon your present blessings -of which every man has many- not on your past misfortunes, of which all men have some."
> —CHARLES DICKENS, ENGLISH WRITER

When resources diminish around us, it creates harmony. It teaches us a lesson that there must be balance. If we always and continually received everything we wanted, then we'd not understand the joys of receiving. We'd stop celebrating our successes and wins and continually move on to the next want and leave our joys behind.

> "He who lives in harmony with himself lives in harmony with the universe."
> —Marcus Aurelius, Roman leader

Comparing yourself and your lives to others is a favorite pastime of humans. Here you compare your weakness to the strength of someone else. At worst you make these comparisons based on incomplete information and inaccurate perceptions.

Here's an example: I have a friend, he's incredible social and outgoing. He enters a situation and not only does he connect with people, but he also brings energy and life to the interaction. I wanted to be like him, but felt that I wasn't like him nor could ever be— "it just wasn't me." These actions and thoughts robbed me of joys, my progress, and left me feeling less competent, then I held myself back. Only when I started learning from him, moving past my fears and speaking up did I see I already had the traits I respected in him. I just had to use them.

> "What are you costing yourself by not giving 100 percent?"

Over time, as you continually compare yourself to others, you'll always come up short. Instead of focusing on your small wins and growth, the increased likelihood is a path that slows down your achievement of sweet dreams.

> "Why are you so enchanted by this world, when a mine
> of gold lies within you?"
> —RUMI, PERSIAN POET

Is it challenging for you to see that you already have enough? To understand and celebrate what is in your life. Stop waiting for others to throw a party for you. You can throw your own. Know the world has everything you need, and when you're ready to move towards it, all is available. I'm rich in life because I choose to celebrate what I have.

> "Think not so much of what you lack as of what you have: but of
> the things that you have, select the best, and then reflect on how
> eagerly you would have sought them if you did not have them."
> –MARCUS AURELIUS, ROMAN LEADER, *MEDITATIONS*

Find abundance in your life; your future is greater than you give it credit for, and it is waiting for you to move forward with focus and self-kindness. The first step is to focus and give thanks for what you have in life. Second step, share with others (your knowledge, experience, some of your resources), and they will also create more abundance in the world. By me creating more for you, I create more for me and everyone around us.

Bottom Line for Wisdom is the Beginning: If you focus your entire life on lack, guess what you'll feel your entire life? Lack. At some point you must realize that the view of lack is not serving you well.

Wisdom is the Beginning Personal Activity: What is one unhealthy habit that has cost you the most? What would you gain by removing it from your life and replacing it with a habit of acknowledging abundance?

Self-Limiting:
Life Out of Balance

Life's Challenge: Keep life in balance. Some see this as impossible, others have never considered it, and more don't even want it. Life can and will become out of balance frequently. It is a conscious choice when you bring it back to your life. First, make it a conscious choice and don't just allow yourself to live that way. Second, understand that life works best when balance is present.

What is a balanced life? It's one where there is an equilibrium in the essential areas of your life—family, work, learning, social, spiritual, giving, to name a few. There is a set amount of time, and by adding time to one are of your life, another area will be left with less, and it will suffer. An out-of-balance life becomes bumpy and the ride uncomfortable.

The most common example in our society is an out of whack work-life balance. By working 10 or 12 hours a day, my duties (to myself and others) must be passed along.

This can be to any number of individuals: spouse, children, friends, parents. I work a bit too long so I show up late for a dinner with a friend. I work the weekend and have to renegotiate one-on-one time with my son. I work and leave the home life to my spouse to take care of all alone. It will get bumpy over time and relationships will suffer. The more balance I lose, the more agreements I break because of the situation I've created.

Wisdom is the Beginning: Normally this is how it takes place, when life is out of balance. You give up balance to have more x (you fill in the x: money, feeling of importance, escape etc.). As you receive the material possession or feeling of being momentarily rewarded and focus more time and resources to have more x, you'll continue to take from other areas of your life. That move makes your life a bit more out of balance. At first it is slightly noticed (maybe even encouraged by others), but as time passes, other areas of your life desire or even demand more of your time and attention; then over a long time span of weeks or months, you may lose aspects of life that you've ignored. Only then is it understood that "success" isn't about money, prestige, power. It is about finding your balance in life. It is about overall success in all areas, not just one. If I fail my son and don't create time for him, then all the success in another area won't make up for it.

Why do individuals choose to live an out-of-balance life? There is a pay-off, of course! The pay-off for the individual living an out-of-balance life, such as working too many hours, is professional prestige, better finances, a feeling of success. For the individual who is focused on a life of recreation, the pay-off might be lower stress and plenty of down time. The individual who gives their time away gains societal prestige and a full schedule. While there is a pay-off, there is also a price.

"There is nothing so terrible as activity without insight."
—Johann Wolfgang von Goethe, German poet

Typically, two areas suffer the most when we live out of balance 1) Family, and 2) Health. This situation leads to fewer life-long memories and often a shortened life. These are two of the most important areas of your life. Without them, your wins are muted. Without family by your side, your earned prestige cannot be shared. Without your health, life is shortened and/or dampened.

"God gave us the gift of life; it is up to us to give ourselves the gift of living well."
—Voltaire, French writer

The additional challenge with living an out-of-balance life is once you've set it up, it is a challenge to adjust the expectations of those around you. You've taught them how you want to be treated. What is important to you, once you make a change, is that too often others don't understand or appreciate it. All too often their life is also out of balance, so it may back them up to see a step toward a healthy lifestyle.

> "If you do not change direction, you may end up where you are heading."
> —Lao Tzu, Chinese philosopher

Be conscious and purposeful with your time and choices, if you set your life on cruise-control and it is out of balance, then it will keep heading down the road exactly as you left it. Look into your future. What will the next five years of your life hold? Not exactly what you're doing today. Fortunately, and unfortunately, it will hold **more** of where you're focusing your energy.

As those five years pass and the pressures of your choices build, other areas weaken and are drained. At some point those areas start to "rebel." They are giving you information that things must change; they are providing feedback. Your family speaks up and asks for more from you. Your health gives out a little, then a lot. The price must be paid at this point. Of course, it can be ignored for a time, but in the end, life will extract its balance. The longer delayed, the bigger, more impactful, and more painful, the price that will be paid.

> "Beware the barrenness of a busy life."
> —Socrates, Greek philosopher

Choose to never be too busy; instead develop your true talents. You lose every time you become too busy and allow it to take you away from what you desire to have. It is easy to fill life with busy work to feel important, while what is important to you is lost.

If you weren't busy for the purpose of being busy, with what would your life be filled? Would you fill it with passions? Would you find new interests? Would you increase the peace you feel? Who, outside yourself, would benefit the most from your quality time?

Many who are "too busy" don't understand the word *no* and don't understand the world will not end if the word is respectfully uttered. It is often believed to be a bad word, feeling that others will lose respect for you. The truth is that without healthy boundaries, you lose yourself.

"It is not enough to be busy. So are the ants. The question is:
What are you busy about?"
—HENRY DAVID THOREAU, AMERICAN ESSAYIST

Stop allowing a busy life to run every second of your day. What kind of life does that lead to in 5 or 10 years? Perhaps getting what you want starts with sitting, resting and thinking. That or continue to do the same, and do what you've always done, arriving at the same ending.

"DO JUST ONE THING AT A TIME."

Bottom Line for Wisdom is the Beginning: I personally cannot claim a successful life without my family, without my peers, without feeling healthy, without giving back, without learning, without financial resources, and without inner peace and balance. My friends and family want my quality time. When I lose sight of this, I also lose sight of the opportunity to deepen and strengthen the most important part of my life.

> "What lies behind you, and what lies in front of you, pales in comparison to what lies inside you."
> —RALPH WALDO EMERSON, AMERICAN WRITER

Wisdom is the Beginning Personal Activity: What is truly important? Find some time to answer the question for yourself. Then align your time and priorities so they work together. Don't allow society to convince you of your priorities; this leads to unfulfillment.

Self-Limiting: Waiting for life to happen

Life's Challenge: Life can tempt—the lottery, becoming a billionaire at 25, fairytales, romantic comedies. Life tempts us into fully believing that life-changing "magical moments" are just around that corner, waiting for us to just show up, then all will be wonderful. We have proof as we've seen it happen online and on television.

He won 100 million in the lottery. She became a billionaire before 30. A whole movie industry and book business built on someone appearing in your life and taking you to greatness or true love. It does happen, but it is completely out of your control, so don't sit and wait until it shows up. Focus on what is in your control and amazing things will happen.

Wisdom is the Beginning: You want something mesmerizing in your life, or for your life. Most want to have many different material and non-material items and experiences in life. How you go about obtaining, or waiting to obtain them, is a huge dividing point for those who have, and experience for those who are still waiting.

> "Everybody wants to be somebody; nobody wants to grow."
> —JOHANN WOLFGANG VON GOETHE, GERMAN POET

Fortunately, the equation to have these items in your life is easy enough. The unfortunate truth is that you must self-motivate to obtain. Many want those material or non-material items, but they don't want to do what it takes to get them. Understand what you want, then commit to do what it takes to achieve your goal. Consider the analogy that seeds are impossible to see below the ground, and some plants take years to bear fruit.

> "To see things in the seed, that is genius."
> —LAO TZU, CHINESE PHILOSOPHER

There is no promise that you'll ever obtain exactly what you desire, whatever that may be, but it is likely you'll end up close to that point. However, the true fulfillment comes from the personal commitment to achieve it. With persistence towards a goal and dream, I cannot promise when you'll arrive, but I will promise that you'll arrive.

> "If we are facing in the right direction, all we have to do is keep on walking."
> —BUDDHIST PROVERB

How and where to begin is often the toughest part of the experience. Every success in life starts in your mind. You must know your target before you can begin the path, or at times it is simply a matter of starting to walk. Once you have your target, take one step towards it. Often the journey seems too distant and too unknown, and so taking one step in that direction gets you a small win. There is no way around it, except through it.

Without starting, there will never be an arrival. Keep taking the next step, if you're stuck and not sure of your next best action. Ask a trusted friend or mentor for input. Outside points of view can be refreshing, while relying solely on internal knowledge limits you to a small fraction of the brilliance available.

"The secret of getting ahead is getting started."
—MARK TWAIN, AMERICAN WRITER

Circle back to the opening of this chapter. Many people want glory, love, success, power and more, but few are willing to make it happen. It is infinitely easier to hope someone does it for you and thrust it upon your life. You are living the life you created, and chances are no one will place opportunities in your lap. If you don't like the life you have, then do something different. If you want more, then do more.

"WISHING IT, WANTING IT AND DOING IT ARE VERY DIFFERENT THINGS."

Remember big payoffs take big risks. What are you willing to give and do for your wildest dreams to come true? The bigger the dream, the longer the road to arrival, and the greater the sacrifice along the way. So think wisely: what got you here is not getting you there.

> "The bold adventurer succeeds the best."
> —OVID, ROMAN POET

I appreciate people who live their dreams and "go for it" in their lives. I choose to seek them out and create relationship with them. It motivates me and drives me forward in my dreams. I look to them because, on many levels, I respect and emulate them when I find a characteristic I want in my life.

Be very cautious about how you judge yours and others' successes by appearance. Their road was not always easy, nor were they always on top. Learn from it all.

"ARE YOU HERE TO GIVE IT YOUR ALL OR JUST WATCH?"

Hard work and self-care (mentally and emotionally) lead to tremendous opportunities and events taking place in your life. When people see what you are doing, they help you do more. When I know someone is working toward a goal, then I'm open to playing a part to assist them. Their motivation is contagious. It is a blessing to have it in my life. Consider this small example: when I see children working their lemonade stand, I do my best to stop and buy a glass. I know there are many lessons to learn for their life though self-motivation. What do you think or do when you find someone on their way in life who asks for assistance?

Bottom Line for Wisdom is the Beginning: Now is the biggest motivator you have in life. The motto of "I'll do it tomorrow" or "I'll do it soon" can be repeated again and again. Now is all you have; take your next best step towards a big dream.

"The only person you are destined to become is the person you decide to be."
—Ralph Waldo Emerson, American writer

Self-Limiting: Guilt

Life's Challenge: What is the reason for guilt in our lives? What function does it hold?

Do you consider yourself an overall good or bad person? Most believe, overall, they are good. Therefore, how do you handle situations where you define your actions as bad? This is where guilt enters the picture. It has little, if any, use in your life and often people implement it as a form of punishment.

> "No amount of guilt will change the past..."
> —UMAR IBN AL-KHATTAB, HISTORICAL FIGURE

Guilt is understandable; the danger comes when we don't clear it out and forgive, or we relive the past and the guilt builds. This situation can cause huge issues in life and drag us down. With guilt we often misuse the memory of the past and waste the opportunity to learn from it.

Wisdom is the Beginning:

"One minute of patience can result in ten years of peace."
—GREEK PROVERB

What good has come out of your guilt? It may push you to self-correct your path. Another potential benefit is to learn the lesson and move on. Unfortunately, the easiest tripping point is to feel the guilt, then refuse to move on. Normally it is not used as a chance to improve, rather a time to beat yourself up again and again.

"When the past calls, let it go to voice mail. Believe me, it has nothing new to say."
—UNKNOWN

Does your guilt work for you? No! Then do anything healthy to create learning and movement to clear it out. Sitting in it is a horrible option. The only person who has the power to do anything about past guilt is the person creating the guilt—you. Find closure, apologize (to others and yourself), and work on forgiveness.

"Man is free at the moment he wishes to be."
—VOLTAIRE, FRENCH WRITER

The longer you hold onto past actions, the less you live in the now and prepare for a better future. Every single individual has taken part in a situation which they look back and regret. What does that mean for you?

"GUILT IS NEVER POSITIVE."

You have choices, however. As long as you feed your guilt, all you'll receive is more guilt. Acknowledge that you "messed that up" and commit to doing it differently next time. Also recognize that you're a better person today because of what you've learned. Don't live in the guilt.

"Certain defects are necessary for the existence of individuality."
—JOHANN WOLFGANG VON GOETHE, GERMAN POET

Would your best friend want you to feel guilty? Not likely. Does your partner want you to be free of the weight of past actions? Yes. Do you want the children in your life to have the ability to look at the past and forgive errors? Surely, yes. Who is the hardest judge of your past acts? You're the toughest one. Everyone of your loved ones wants you to release the guilt and be free. Defects and mistakes are necessary to develop character—your character.

"Nothing is more wretched than the mind of a man conscious of guilt."
—PLAUTUS, ROMAN PLAYWRIGHT

The most powerful weapon you have against guilt is action. Where does action take place? In the now. Guilt draws you into the past; it wants you to live in the past. When you force yourself into action, it moves your mind into the present and you start to live more fully. Of course, your mind will wander back into the past, back to guilt. When you find yourself there, then take back control of your thoughts.

"Where guilt is, rage and courage doth abound."
—BEN JOHNSON, ENGLISH PLAYWRIGHT

Do I have actions that I regret? Certainly, I can easily move into a guilty frame of mind. We all have places in our past that are heavy and regretful. We've all hurt others, made poor judgment calls, and inflicted pain on ourselves. It is normal to have ugly pieces in our past; it is part of growth.

"He who lives without folly isn't so wise as he thinks."
—FRANCOIS DE LA ROCHEFOUCAULD, FRENCH WRITER
AND MEMOIRIST

Take note, never feel guilty about feeling guilty. This is a useless state. Imagine the amount of energy wasted about feeling double guilt. If guilt doesn't work for you, then imagine how useless it is feeling guilt about guilt. Dump that useless guilt into the nearest wastebasket.

"Next to the dog, the wastebasket is man's best friend."
—ANONYMOUS

Bottom Line for Wisdom is the Beginning: Let it begin with the phrase "I forgive...." It may be for a moment, and when the guilt resurfaces, return to "I forgive...." Over time the forgiveness builds until one day the memory is just like telling a story; there is no longer the sting of emotion linked to it.

"Life is thickly sown with thorns, and I know no other remedy than to pass quickly through them. The longer we dwell on our misfortunes, the greater is their power to harm us."
—VOLTAIRE, FRENCH WRITER

Wisdom is the Beginning Personal Activity: First, who's truly guilty in the situation that brings you down and makes it impossible to let go of your past? If it is the other individual, then steps must be taken to work towards forgiveness. If it is you, then be accountable and apologize. There are many ways to apologize—verbal or written, for example. Maybe it isn't appropriate or safe to say the words face to face or send the written apology, however, that should not stop you from saying the words to yourself or to a trusted friend, or writing the letter (maybe to never send it).

Life is Inharmonic

Life's Challenge: Some of the biggest questions in life don't have all-encompassing answers. What is the meaning of life? Why does it bring us challenges? Why is there pain? There are answers for each and every person. There is no one answer for all.

When looking for answers, make sure you're asking the right questions. Ensure that you're asking questions that can be answered. You might need to look at the problem from a new point of view or with a new set of knowledge. The better question you ask yourself, the better answer you'll find.

Wisdom is the Beginning: What is the reason for your current situation in life? Are you satisfied with the state of your relationships? How about your financial situation, friendships, and spiritual growth? What about your learning? The more time you spend on contemplation of your past, and why your present doesn't look as wonderful as another individual's, you're falling into the trap of uselessly criticizing yourself without action. Stop condemning yourself for your view of other's actions which took place long ago.

"Each player must accept the cards life deals him or her: but once they are in hand, he or she alone must decide how to play the cards in order to win the game."
—Voltaire, French writer

The actions of comparing, condemning and complaining create larger and larger walls between yourself and some of the most important relationships in your lives. It is logical to have built the walls long ago to protect your younger self, but often you forget that you can take them down. You have the power to re-evaluate your current relationships and let go of the past. With your walls growing bigger, thicker, and taller every day, you block out not only the pain, but also the joy, love and relationship you desire.

"Our task is not to seek for love, but merely to seek and find all the barriers within yourself that you have built against it."
—Rumi, Persian poet

The unhealed pains of your past, and the resentment you carry into today, are the most powerful hindrance to feeling love. This is true not only in love found in your closest relationships but also in your friendships. The walls and unhealed pains of your past can play a role in holding you back from your dreams. It can be encountered in your learning and growth. In order for you to move forward, you must clear out the past and keep it clear as you go.

"Life is too short to be little. Man is never so manly as when he feels deeply, acts boldly, and expresses himself with frankness and with fervor."
—BENJAMIN DISRAELI, BRITISH STATESMAN

You want to do something great in life. Where you are now can be okay, but there is more. The biggest barrier to obtaining whatever it is you desire is yourself. You must find a manner to get out of your own way.

"Whatever you can do, or dream you can, begin it. Boldness has genius, power and magic in it."
—ATTRIBUTED TO JOHANN WOLFGANG VON GOETHE, GERMAN POET

Use your incredibly powerful mind and logic to find the question that best leads the search for your answers on what holds you back in life. Once you have the best question possible, your brain will seek the answer. Does it involve a past action of your own or someone else's action that affected you? Does it involve distance in a current relationship or a lack of commitment? Does it involve a shallowness of feelings? These inquiries will lead you to deep answers where healing can take place. Push the need to lay blame out of your mind.

Life brings pain.
Life brings challenges.
Your role in life is to bring joy to you. This will bring joy to others, in turn.
Everyone must learn what is in their control and what is not. Immediately stop blaming others for things that happen; to blame is fruitless. Immediately stop making excuses and playing small.

In the following chapters consider your beliefs about life, here's what will be covered:
- Life should be fair
- Anything worthwhile will take more work than you think
- Being alone sadness

Life should be fair

Life's Challenge: We all want a fair shake at life and in any given situation. We want everyone to have a fair chance at building their success. We want things to be fair, yet we know things are not always fair; that is a key part of the challenge we all face.

Where we become tripped up is when we think this situation should be fair (or more fair). This will cause us a world of hurt; some matters are out of our control, but we can play our part in fairness. We can act in a fair manner to others, and we can seek it in our life. Life is not always perfect, wonderful or fair.

Wisdom is the Beginning: We know that life is not fair (nor perfect, nor wonderful at all times). We live in a mild state of guardedness so that others don't take advantage of us in our transactions. We can become bitter when we do "everything right" and it all turns out wrong. "That was not fair" often leads to increasing unhappiness, suspicion, guardedness, and so on.

A lot of energy is spent thinking about fairness. Continue the fight for fairness in your life, but remove the expectation, because otherwise you'll be disappointed. Move to a mindset of you can handle what enters your space, if it's fair or not.

"We all have enough strength to endure the misfortune of others."
—FRANCOIS DE LA ROCHEFOUCAULD, FRENCH WRITER AND MEMOIRIST

It's not fair that life is unfair, but your interpretation and response is the key. In the end, you have complete control over your reaction to the situation and individual. This is where you can instill power and create the life you desire. How do you want to be seen in the world? Powerful? Successful? Authentic? Confident? There is your map forward into challenging situations.

"If the wind will not serve, take to the oars."
—LATIN PROVERB

The most powerful individual you can become is to accept what happens in any situation and take it for your strength. When life is good, seize the moment and push it to great! When life is down, seize the moment, create value and grow. As in the quote, if the wind is not blowing in the direction you hoped, you can use the oars and steer your boat in the direction you desire.

"Happy he who learns to bear what he cannot change."
—FRIEDRICH SCHILLER, GERMAN POET

Maybe life isn't fair or unfair, it is just life. When you move to a place of acceptance, situations can be unfair at times. It's your choice as to what you accept and when you choose to engage in the situation. At this point you take control. You can decide to let some things go that would cause further distress.

"Learn to let go. That is the key to happiness."
—BUDDHA, PHILOSOPHER

Life is often judged as unfair when you don't get what you want out of a situation or individual. You think you deserve the raise or promotion. "I must have x" or "If I just had x, then my life would be elevated." Don't lose sight of the fact that that 7 billion people have a similar thought. Fairness changes perspective quickly when others are factored into the equation. Consider what you want more of in your life time—possessions or feelings. This is a fantastic starting place to start and determine where to focus your energies.

"Happiness resides not in possessions, and not in gold, happiness dwells in the soul."
—DEMOCRITUS, GREEK PHILOSOPHER

The unfortunate truth is that you don't have all the information. You don't know what people are thinking, nor the true heart of their actions. You are capable of taking a huge step to understand their point of view and to give them the benefit of the doubt, but you only know your intentions when you ask or see (and judge) their actions.

On these facts, you judge fairness. Acknowledge you have insufficient information. Be aware how far down the road you are and how much power you give your sole perception.

> "Life is the art of drawing sufficient conclusions
> from insufficient premises."
> —SAMUEL BUTLER, BRITISH POET

You must put aside your beliefs about life, that it must be fair and that life is fair. You must live in "life is inharmonic" and know your perception at times is fair, and other times it is not. You must deal with what is. If an unfair person enters, you can engage with them on a level in which you are comfortable, or you can disengage. If you conduct business with an organization that is unethical, you can set up your boundaries or find the next supplier. You can forgive and move on, or you can become increasingly frustrated.

"They that apply themselves to trifling matters commonly
become incapable of great ones."
—FRANCOIS DE LA ROCHEFOUCAULD, FRENCH WRITER AND
MEMOIRIST

Focus your life on big personal goals and know that
others' actions are outside your control. Know that all
you can do is keep your integrity intact and make your
dealings fair.

"THERE ARE TIMES WHEN WE MUST DEAL WITH WHAT IS."

Bottom Line for Wisdom is the Beginning: I trust that if
the situation arises where my trust was misplaced in people
who surround me, I will become increasingly aware of
that individual's actions. I want people in my life who are
fair and act with integrity. Once that trust is broken, and
no steps are taken to repair the error, I'll create distance. I
can choose who I allow into my life and to what extent. I
choose to not allow "unfair" individuals.

"I ask not for a lighter burden, but for broader shoulders."
—JEWISH PROVERB

Wisdom is the Beginning Personal Activity: Examine
who makes up the rules about life. No doubt you've
received your moral bearing (or lack of) from your parents/
family/upbringing. Also, religious and society institutions

play a significant role for most people. In these lessons and rules, you'll find your personal definition of what is and isn't fair. Dissect and examine your moral code and understand where it is (and isn't) true for you.

It will take more than you think

Life's Challenge: We all have, or had, dreams to be billionaires. Some of us want to be business moguls. Others want the ideal family. Some individuals want the most expensive car, while others want to be the most respected in the field of choice. No matter what your desire, it will take longer than you expect. It will seem you're ready for it long before it happens.

The biggest challenge is to continue to walk in faith that your dreams are obtainable, even if life is sending messages that make you doubt. Keep focus on your heart's desire when there's no assurance of arrival time or date.

Wisdom is the Beginning: Now is the only time there is in life. Do you have the exact relationship you want? Do you have the level of income? Do you have the depth of spiritual knowledge you desire, and the lifestyle? Do you

Gregory B. Davis

have the housing? Do you have the friends? The only time to start to have those is now.

"Success depends upon previous preparation and without such preparation there is sure to be failure."
—CONFUCIUS, CHINESE PHILOSOPHER

Your daily habits determine what kind of individual you are, will become, and what success you'll taste in life. Look at how you spend your time, and this will show you what type of life you'll have in the future. Your habits (when no one is looking) create your future. Your mental habits create and control your physical habits, which create your life.

"Without continual growth and progress, such words as improvement, achievement and success have no meaning."
—BENJAMIN FRANKLIN, FOUNDING FATHER OF US DECLARATION OF INDEPENDENCE

Continual self-improvement is the key to an incredibly successful life. You must work on yourself in order to create the greatness you wish to see within yourself. Now is the only time there is in your life. Start now on what you want. Stop filling your life with deterring habits and procrastination.

"What is not started today is never finished tomorrow."
—JOHANN WOLFGANG VON GOETHE, GERMAN POET

The first time is difficult. The first step of the first time you do something new is the most difficult. However, that first step is vital. Without it, nothing happens. Nothing happens with your idea, nothing happens in your life, now or in your future. Preparing to step is a slippery path, but you can prepare your life away waiting for the perfect plan.

"The first step, my son, which one makes in the world, is the one on which depends the rest of our days."
—VOLTAIRE, FRENCH WRITER

Unfortunately, when I examine many of my "first steps" and what was going on mentally, I understand where it led me in the short and long term. I see, over and over, how I missed out on much by delaying my first step (and after that delayed first step, delaying my next best step). Often I didn't focus on the next option, and I became distracted or moved into my fears. How I lose the most is by doing nothing. When I take a step that doesn't work, or I lose time, I still learn. When I do nothing, nothing happens. No progress, no learning takes place to move me toward my next dream.

Right now, in this very moment, decide to take that first step or continue on with the next one if you're stuck.

"The best time to plant a tree was 20 years ago.
The second best time is now."
—CHINESE PROVERB

Now and then again tomorrow, take another step ....
What you're doing is creating your habits. You're preparing
yourself for the next opportunity, and the next one you
desire. Always move forward and create more of what you
want. Your habits can assist or rob you of creating what you
want in life.

"It is not easy, but it is worth it."
—UNKNOWN

Be very aware of where you focus your mind. By
continuing to focus on the challenges, distractions, let-
downs and roadblocks, you'll only see more. Additionally,
you'll miss your wins and your progress. If it is important
to you and your life, then focus on the path to get to the
peak, and then celebrate on the peak after obtaining it.

"On all the peaks lies peace."
—JOHANN WOLFGANG VON GOETHE, GERMAN POET

It won't be necessarily easy, and it won't happen
"today," but the payoff will be immense when you arrive.
Get started on your goal, take another step toward it. Each
time you move toward it, you will give yourself another
set of improved options for the situation/goal. What more
motivation do you need to see and obtain a dream that will
be with you every day of your life?

Bottom Line for Wisdom is the Beginning: Now, right now, is the only time that exists. When I was a teen, I went to summer camp in the North East U.S. As a Texas boy, hiking in the mountains was not something I knew much about. I recall not feeling very excited about taking multiple day/night trips into the Appalachian Mountains. However, today mostly I recall the feeling of reaching the peak of Mt. Washington, sitting with my friends enjoying a candy bar on top of multiple peaks and feeling physically successful.

What do you want to achieve? What is your goal? Take your next best step, then your next best step, and you'll reach powerfully big goals and create memories to reflect upon the rest of your life.

Wisdom is the Beginning Personal Activity: Decide on your commitment level to the project or task. If your level is below an 8, 9, or 10, then there are two decisions. Is this a true desire and wish for your life? If so, find a way to move up the commitment ladder. If it is not, then release that goal for a future date or never. Focus your life on where you have the most passion and commitment.

Being Alone

Life's Challenge: Earlier in my life I joined an international development organization (the US Peace Corps) overseas working with small businesses. The attrition rate during training, I was told, was 30 percent. I found that to be true. Once training was over and the work began, once again I was told, that an additional 30 percent of applicants would quit. That means more than half of the people walking in the door on day one would not get past the discomfort of the newness and start the project. I often pondered the reason for such a high attrition rate. I believe the number one reason was that people felt alone and were uncomfortable with being solitary.

Today, there is no alone time unless you are purposeful and go to great lengths to create it. We are surrounded by entertainment and devices that fill every single waking moment, if we allow it. We cannot get away from opportunities for distraction from our own thoughts. Cell phones, television, shopping, billboards, advertisements, email, messages, tablets, media, movies, applications—

all wanting our eyes, minds and time. All making it as enjoyable as possible so you return as quickly as possible in every free moment.

This world only compounds the perceived feeling of being alone, versus the benefits. Do you look for opportunities to be alone in peace and silence? Do you fill every second of your day with distractions?

There is a life-long benefit to being comfortable with yourself and a life-long debt to pay for trying to escape yourself at all times. Wherever you go, no matter how fast, you take yourself with you, and there you'll be.

Wisdom is the Beginning: What is the reason you turn your back on spending time alone? What is it about silence that is so powerful? What do you cost yourself by filling every moment with a distraction?

By nature, your brain will focus on what problem/s need to be addressed in your life. Furthermore, brains are rarely quiet; they are constantly working and thinking about how to solve problems and will focus on the biggest issue or the one that's been around the longest.

They are powerful problem-solving machines and incredible at the job. The down side is when you are alone, your mind will drift to problems that need to be addressed. Frequently, a portion of these problems are from your past that you would just as soon forget.

"You already have the world's most advanced creation: your
mind. Use it to create your own miracles."
—ATTICUS, ANCIENT PHILOSOPHER

Once you move into silence, your brain has time
to focus on what is most pressing and important at that
moment. Most people don't have issue with this at first,
or for a short period of time. However, as time passes, the
thoughts become more profound and complex. I believe
this is exactly what led to the attrition of the international
development volunteers in my time with Peace Corps.
The alone time and lack of outside distraction at first
was manageable, however as time passed, their thoughts
became deeper as they reflected on their past unresolved
difficulties or challenges in life.

"To dare to live alone is the rarest courage; since there are many
who had rather meet their bitterest enemy in the field, than their
own hearts in their closet."
—CHARLES CALEB COLTON, ENGLISH WRITER

Until you clear out the difficulties and challenges of
your past, they remain. That is why your brain will focus
and refocus when you move into silence. On most levels,
it is unenjoyable to relive the painful past. However, that
is exactly what the brain will do, with the goal to solve the
past problem or find a new way forward.

Gregory B. Davis

The biggest benefit of all is to allow solitary time and brain focus to bring a solution and potential healing to the past. It is an uncomfortable process to go through. We often steer away from pain rather than greeting it and allowing a solution. Alas, as long as we divert our sight and mind, the brain will return to the issue.

"All men's misfortunes spring from their hatred of being alone."
—Jean de la Bruyère, French satiric moralist

On the other side of feeling comfortable in your alone time is peace. When you never allow yourself to sit alone in silence, your past builds and lacks an outlet. As the Jean de la Bruyère quote suggests, there is a big down side to not cleaning up your past. One of them is your avoidance of alone time.

"True happiness... Arises, in the first place from the enjoyment of one's self."
—Joseph Addison, English essayist and poet

There are enormous benefits to creating alone time and then dealing with your past. Being alone has power—few can handle it, even society. People often think there must be something wrong when someone wants to be alone. When a child reads at a family gathering, or an adult chooses to not attend a night out, others think they are antisocial or a loner,as though something is wrong with them.

Aloneness is not encouraged, stillness is not given time to happen, and down time is seen as a wasted opportunity. Thus we fear it, and we don't encourage it. We fill it for our children, and we fill it for ourselves. People are uncomfortable with others being alone and will try to fill that silence. This practice teaches us to seek outside stimuli and interaction and moves us away from knowing ourselves. The benefits of aloneness are immense. Embrace it.

"BEING ALONE IS THE BEST VITAMIN FOR THE SOUL."

You connect with others to the level that you can connect with yourself. You are only capable of giving away what you have inside yourself. If you're content within yourself, you can offer insight and peace with past challenges. If your past is rocky and unsettled, then it is unlikely that alone time will be embraced, and in multiple ways, those around you will pick up on this attribute. For those who choose to find peace with the past and heaviness of their solo moments, it can be beneficial in work, creativity, and peace of mind.

"What progress, you ask, have I made? I have begun
to be a friend to myself."
—SENECA, ROMAN PHILOSOPHER

Just imagine the inner strength that is provided when you're completely comfortable and confident with who you are and your decisions. You can stand up to anyone and be open with who you are and what you bring; that's beauty and power.

> "THE MORE WE LOVE OURSELVES, THE EASIER
> IT IS TO LOVE OTHERS."

Just because you're alone doesn't necessarily mean you're lonely. The truth is that you are never ever alone, there is never true silence. You have people all around you, ready to be by your side. Only if you want to feel alone is it true. You're only lonely when you choose to create lack of relationship in your life, and one reason you can lack relationship is that you don't have it with yourself.

"YOU ARE ALONE BECAUSE YOU CHOOSE TO FEEL THAT WAY."

Bottom Line for Wisdom is the Beginning: I challenge you to create silence in your life. Start with five minutes a day. Allow your brain to drift and explore. At first it may go to your to-do list or what's for dinner type of thoughts. As the days pass, allow yourself to go deeper and discover what is left to heal in your past. Who deserves more of your attention? What priority needs to be realigned? What is your future dream state? What is your purpose in life?

> "The secret of happiness, you see, is not found in seeking more,
> but in developing the capacity to enjoy less."
> —SOCRATES, GREEK PHILOSOPHER

Sadness

Life's Challenge: Sadness exists and has impacted all of our lives and will continue to do so in our lives going forward. What is the reason it exists? What is the reason some have more of it in their lives? Why do some deal with it better than others? Does it balance joy? Does it allow us to see and know the highs of life? Does it teach lessons? Is it a manner in which to correct our lives?

I have no answers for those excellent questions. I know that it exists and, if allowed, it can take over people's lives. I know that it is necessary to feel sadness and then work your way through it. I know that it is a dangerous position to stay stuck in sadness.

> "My life is a struggle."
> —VOLTAIRE, FRENCH WRITER

Examine what you do with sadness when it enters your life. How do you move out of it? How do you use it to reach those new highs? First and most important, you absolutely can't stay where you are, you can't stay stuck. Allowing the feelings (don't avoid the sadness) and moving forward are the only options.

Keep in mind that internal problems require internal solutions. With sadness you only have the option to seek healing internally. When you resort to external solutions, the core issue is left untended and sadness continues to exist.

Wisdom is the Beginning: Honesty is the place to begin. When you are not emotionally honest with yourself and those around you, you rob yourself of a fabulous opportunity to start to heal. Without honesty, you'll be stuck the rest of your life.

"BE EMOTIONALLY HONEST WITH YOURSELF."

The longer you keep sadness internal, without exploring and sharing what makes/made you sad, it sits in your stomach and drags you down. How can you move from that place? Is counseling an option? What can you do to alleviate the sadness in a positive way? How do you work through it to a better state? The ultimate goal is to find the life lesson and create value for yourself today and in the future from the past sadness.

"Good humor is the health of the soul, sadness is its poison."
—PHILIP STANHOPE, 4TH EARL OF CHESTERFIELD,
BRITISH STATESMAN

The most damaging part of sadness is that it seeps into other areas of your life and can cause enormous problems. Innocent bystanders are caught off guard by their loved one who's never worked to heal their sadness. Share your sadness with your loved ones; it can create stronger relationships in life. The absolute truth is that everyone is sad at times; it is good news as it means you care. Don't ever let it take over your life. Allow sadness to enter, share it, then wish it on its way. For some who have clinical depression (or other biological reasons), then outside support is a must to handle the sadness.

"Life is a series of natural and spontaneous changes. Don't resist them—that only creates sorrow. Let reality be reality. Let things flow naturally forward in whatever way they like."
—LAO TZU, CHINESE PHILOSOPHER

On some level, you can choose to be happy or sad, you alone are responsible. Of course, it is sad that "it" happened to you. The sadness was not deserved, that is in the past. You must decide how long it lives in your life. You must decide what to do with it now. All is within you.

"Nothing is miserable unless you think it so; and on the other hand, nothing brings happiness unless you are content with it."
—BOETHIUS, ROMAN PHILOSOPHER

Time heals, however, I take offence to the saying "this too shall pass." While I agree with the statement, that it is too passive, it will pass if you ignore it, but it is **never gone.** If you face it and own it, and change it into a place of learning and value, then it will pass forever and become something you can use. Once sadness has entered, if you allow time to simply pass and never heal, then there it will stay forever. Forever it will be a place of sadness.

For those who have experienced incredibly tragic events which few can comprehend nor even conceive, there will be sad moments forever. I recall my father telling me that my grandfather was deeply wounded when my cousin died as a young man. My grandfather kept saying at the funeral (and after); "A grandfather should never outlive his grandchild."

The answer for this type of pain is individualistic. It might be to help others in similar circumstances, such as a new career of support, a foundation, a place of healing. I don't believe it ever completely passed for my grandfather, but it can become less painful and sad.

Go back into the moment and feel the feelings, and work through the sadness. Live in the (uncomfortable) feeling of sadness. Then find the value for you.

> "Sadness flies away on the wings of time."
> —JEAN DE LA FONTAINE, FRENCH POET

Working through the pain must be done in emotional honesty as anyone can portray happiness on the outside, and many do, but it takes a brave soul to create value out of past pains. That is a true champion in life—taking a downer in life and turning it up for yourself.

"You cannot prevent the birds of sadness from passing over your head, but you can prevent their making a nest in your hair."
—CHINESE PROVERB

Heal your wounds. While the scar will remain, there is no longer pain attached to it. Don't see it as they've done me wrong in life, rather see it as a painful life event and now I must rebuild my joy. I must create power from sadness. I must welcome sadness when it returns and allow it to pass and to exit. Life brings sadness, it is not personal.

"Reject your sense of injury and the injury itself disappears."
—MARCUS AURELIUS, ROMAN LEADER

No one can heal the past for you. No matter how powerful or important they are, no one else can release the pain. If that were true, then your loved ones would have done it long ago. It is your choice to let go. And so I say:

"YOUR CHOICE OF A LIFETIME, GET BETTER OR NOT."

By choosing to keep a tight hold of the sadness, there is a huge consequence to your living. You know what it is for you. Whatever word you put on it, it doesn't serve you well. It has a negative interaction with your life and your future. Don't mess up your future with your past, leave your past there.

If you constantly look in the rear-view mirror, you'll never move into the present. While you will reflect on your past and learn from it, take steps to move forward; you deserve a future full of gifts and joys. As long as you keep reading the past chapters of your life. you stay there. It is time to write new chapters.

> "Sadness does not come from bad circumstances.
> It comes from bad thoughts."
> —Unknown

Your life and your thoughts are all within your power. The sadness, the hurt, the focus, the next moment, the reaction; today it is yours. Don't wait for others to say "I'm sorry." Instead give the forgiveness to yourself. The past is in the past, leave it there. It was sad, and now it is over as soon as you decide it to be.

> "You can't carry garbage around and smell like a rose."

Shifting your point of view is one of the most powerful acts available. The clearest example of this is a soccer goal. How much power is there in the point of view? One half of the stadium is screaming for utter joy while the other half sheds tears of pain. It is the same act with the same people involved, and it is incredibly powerful. The only shift is the viewpoint. That same shift must take place inside you to see the value in your past. Freedom is waiting for you. Once you decide to be free and do what it takes to arrive at the destination, your world will be at peace.

"The only way to deal with an unfree world is to become so absolutely free that your very existence is an act of rebellion."
—ALBERT CAMUS, FRENCH PHILOSOPHER

Bottom Line for Wisdom is the Beginning: Avoid focusing on the sadness of the past and bring healing to your life and memories.

Discouragement

Life's Challenge: The inescapable state of discouragement. If you're really living life, really going for it, then of course, you'll find instances of discouragement standing in your way many times, perhaps daily. It's part of pushing the limits of your life and the situation. You'll be run down, people will not appreciate your changes, and you'll face walls that you must understand how to get around.

On the flip side of life, if you've used your free will to do absolutely nothing constructive with your life, you'll also face huge hurdles of discouragement. Getting started on a direction will be a huge challenge to face (mostly internal challenge).

Discouragement is a part of life; it happens to everyone no matter to what extent you are living your life and no matter how well you do.

> "It's not what happens to you, but how you react
> to it that matters."
> —Epictetus, Greek philosopher

People must be aware to what extent they're allowing discouragement to impact their life and path. Discouragement may have started from many different sources (a difficult childhood, a sad memory, a bad decision), but today you're 100 percent responsible for it, as you control the moments of your life. You must change how you view discouragement, learn from it, if applicable, and if not put it aside and keep moving forward.

Wisdom is the Beginning:

"Don't judge each day by the harvest you reap but by the seeds that you plant."
—ROBERT LOUIS STEVENSON, SCOTTISH WRITER

You'll find what you are looking for in life. You see what you choose to see, whether it's good or not. You'll experience accomplishment and have setbacks. You'll have successes and discouragement. It is not one or the other; the fact is both exist and you'll see more of the one you seek.

When I feel discouragement seeping into a situation, I stop and ask myself; "What do I want more of in life?" If conquering the situation is a step toward having more of what I want, then I reset and put forth the effort. If I'm still having issues with discouragement, then I enlist a trusted support person. It is amazing what expressing the goal, roadblock, and desired result can do for motivation.

"Dream no small dreams for they have no power
to move the hearts of men."
—JOHANN WOLFGANG VON GOETHE, GERMAN POET

The easiest viewpoint to undertake is how little you've accomplished and how far you have to go. So much work for so little benefit. So much work to do, and who knows if it will ever pay off. Discouragement is shifting the tide inside of you. The challenge is to see and believe in the future, your payoff for the work you've done today.

"There is no education like adversity."
—BENJAMIN DISRAELI, BRITISH POLITICIAN, NOVELIST,
AND ESSAYIST, SERVING TWICE AS PRIME MINISTER
OF THE UNITED KINGDOM

Discouragement is one of the biggest adversities we will face in life. A project that doesn't work out quite the way you thought it would, or an attempt failed on your goal. You'll recognize it or them in your own life. At times discouragement is feels and appears insurmountable, and at other times, unrelenting. In the end, it is the best teacher. You'll never forget the lessons; you know there is more of it ahead, and (most importantly) you know that it is within your control to move through it and succeed.

"Fresh activity is the only means of overcoming adversity."
—JOHANN WOLFGANG VON GOETHE, GERMAN POET

What are the two basic options available to you once discouragement comes into view? Keep working toward your goals, or allow discouragement to stop you in your tracks? It is a perfect time to take a moment in silence and self-reflect, to examine your dream and goal. When you determine you're on the right track, move discouragement aside and continue.

> "There are two things a person should never be angry at, what they can help, and what they cannot."
> —Plato, Greek philosopher

Beware of the temptation of discouragement, because one of the most tempting states is to blame your dreams away. Blaming is such an effective distraction from reaching your dream. You can blame others (or something) to hide the fact that you are extremely discouraged. You can blame yourself, which never works out well in the end.

> "If you can't catch fish, don't blame the sea."
> —Greek Proverb

Blaming is an option, but it will accomplish nothing. Move to ownership of your challenges and know they are yours to conquer. Living your dreams and goals is a beautiful way forward through challenges. Live your life, because if you don't, few people will be disappointed. When you live life to the fullest, the world will notice and cheer you on.

"Is life not a thousand times too short for us to bore ourselves?"
—Friedrich Nietzsche, German philosopher

Find excitement in the beginning of your journey. Find joy and passion in the middle of the accomplishments. The end is where life's big payoffs come into focus—where your confidence builds, where you find your true purpose in life. Then celebrate, do it in a big way! Many move on to their next goal or dream without taking the time to acknowledge the win. With this celebration, you gain more power to face the next round of discouragement.

"What we are now is not as important
as what we may become."

You'll handle discouragement better as you build on your successes. Success can be from what life demands of us; for me, it was beating cancer. Success can be from what we undertake for ourselves; for me, write multiple books and engage in intense daily exercise. Identify and use all your successes to meet the next round of discouragement.

Find your purpose in life, live your purpose, and discouragement will be insignificant. Additionally, once you put words on your true purpose (mine is simple: lead by helping another find joy), then you have a powerful tool to reach new goals and create more successes.

"He who has not the spirit of this age, has all the misery of it."
—Voltaire, French writer

People often ask me the question, "How do I face and get around discouragement?"

One effective solution is to ask those you trust for their time. Most often when facing discouragement, you may need their input and assistance. It does takes vulnerability on your part.

"It doesn't matter how slowly you go as long as you do not stop."
—Confucius, Chinese philosopher

Allow your mind to open and see amazing things taking place, then move in that direction. When you can't see the beautiful future, your present will be uneventful and full of discouragement.

Often discouragement is intertwined with (lack of) commitment. When I find myself struggling with a project or goal, I grade my level of commitment. If I'm not at a 10, if I'm not 100 percent committed to the task. This is the time I find discouragement arising more easily and more often. Nothing happens in life until I'm a committed 10. If I'm below a 10, I must find a way to move my engagement in that direction, and if I've have decided that a 10 was not possible, I make the conscious decision to move on to the next ambition.

"Every one goes astray, but the least imprudent
are they who repent the soonest."
—Voltaire, French writer

What advice would you give to a friend who's discouraged? Would you let them talk about it and offer to be a sounding board? Often the opportunity to talk about a problem helps the person deal with what is happening. If you can encourage the friend by what has gone well, your friend can keep going in the right direction. It is powerful to learn and then teach from our own and other's experiences in life.

At times removing yourself, even slightly, from the situation will give you the clarity needed to find an answer.

"It is during our darkest moments that we must focus
to see the light."
—Aristotle, Ancient Greek philosopher

There are no complete answers for discouragement, only a shift in mindset and action. You must move forward into the unknown, and when that doesn't work, find another path forward. It will work, life will work with no promises as to how, when, or where you'll end up.

"All life is an experiment. The more experiments
you make the better."
—Ralph Waldo Emerson, American writer

Dream big—your one life deserves it. Whether it's a dream to impact people's lives or buy your first house … It will be exciting! My big dream for this book is that you take one quote, idea, and change in your life that, in a small way, pays big dividends over your lifetime and then contact me and pass along the story.

Bottom Line for Wisdom is the Beginning:

"EVEN WHEN DISCOURAGED, YOU ARE STRONG."

This is your life, and you are the only one who can make it happen. When facing discouragement, use the tools at your disposal to move to the other side.

"Plunge boldly into the thick of life, and seize where you will, it is always interesting."
—JOHANN WOLFGANG VON GOETHE, GERMAN POET

Discouragement is going to happen on the long journey of dreams coming true. You'll face some on your own, some with outside support, and successfully bypass them all. Commitment and focus on the pay-off is your fuel. Successful people do the things others won't do. Go ahead, gather your courage and reach your goal.

"Perfect courage is to do without witnesses what one would be capable of doing with the world looking on."
—Francois de la Rochefoucauld,
French writer and memoirist

Wisdom is the Beginning Personal Activity: We are all discouraged at times; there is no shame in it. The question is how long have you been discouraged and how much power are you giving it over your life. You know where you want to go, and you'll go through discouragement to get there. How much longer will you allow it to be in your way?

Death

Life's Challenge:

"There is a joy in sorrow which none but a mourner can know."
—JEAN PAUL, GERMAN AUTHOR

The thought of death is uncomfortable even for the most faithful, and the thought of the time coming for our closest loved one is almost unbearable. In life, we are not ready for death and at the end of life, we are not often ready for death. While there is no escaping, avoiding, or denying it, death is rarely embraced.

Typically, death is not a welcome thought for anyone at any time in life. Therefore, how can you use it as a mental shift to your advantage? What value can you draw from the fact to lead yourself to a more successful life?

Wisdom is the Beginning: Where are you focusing your energies, on life or on death? Those who choose to focus on death are missing the point of life. The "party" is happening here and now, not at your last breath. Be conscious of your views and focus on the now versus the end. If your focus is on anything but life, then you will give up the opportunity of life right now. If you don't focus on what is important, and in your control, then you'll miss the joys to be found.

"Don't cry because it is over, smile because it happened."
—LUDWIG JACOBOWSKI, GERMAN POET

You've received your deadline. What are you going to do now? You cannot pretend that you have "tomorrow" and "tomorrow" to get started really living life. Your time is up and the clock is counting.

"On neither the sun, nor death, can a man look fixedly."
—FRANCOIS DE LA ROCHEFOUCAULD, FRENCH WRITER
AND MEMOIRIST

Have you considered the math? You get approximately 30,000 days and then, on average, life draws to a close. Of course, none of that is promised. You could get a few hours or a few years. On average you will receive those 30,000 days. Sounds like a lot, but dissect it a bit.

I believe the math is off. From an adult perspective, most people don't start consciously living life until they are 18 (or later), and so at 18 you have 23,400 days. Now you have your deadline. What will your project/s be?

Seeing it as true and you are 30 years old, you have 19,000 days, and if you are 50, you have 11,700 days.

Time becomes short very quickly. Approximately one third of your life has passed at 30 and two thirds at 50. Make no mistake, it is shocking to break it down by days. The thousands of days that have passed are gone, no more to be counted. They can be of use for fond memories and life learnings. The only thing that you have control over are those thousands of days ahead of you. Use them wisely or they will pass just like the days behind you. Life is short.

> "If you realize that all things change, there is nothing
> you will try to hold on to. If you are not afraid of dying,
> there is nothing you cannot achieve."
> —LAO TZU, CHINESE PHILOSOPHER

In truth no one knows how many days are left, but by pretending you have unlimited days, you are doing yourself an injustice. You can squander a great deal of your life. At times it seems as though life is never ending, that you have all the time you want. As I learned at 33 and two close friends learned in their mid-40's, life can change from a future of 30 or 40 or 50 years to "get your lives in order because you have months to live."

The best insight I can share with you is to imagine yourself in the future and look back over your life. What do you see? Wasted time or successes?

> "It is vain for the coward to flee; death follows close behind; it is
> only by defying it that the brave escape."
> —VOLTAIRE, FRENCH WRITER

Give this mental experiment a chance. What if you knew you'd be leaving your town or your friends in a month? How will you spend the time you have left there? What words would you say? For whom would you buy lunch? If you do this with integrity, I guarantee your life will be fuller. Consider saying the words to people in your life. Don't wait until you have a month left with them. Communicate it today what their friendship means to you.

> "Nothing is worth more than this day. You cannot relive yesterday. Tomorrow is still beyond your reach."
> —JOHANN WOLFGANG VON GOETHE, GERMAN POET

Far from being painful, knowing there's an end makes life richer. Embrace the time and live; death will arrive soon enough.

Here is another exercise for you. Write your obituary of your greatest successes to date. Are you satisfied with your life? Now write what you want your greatest life to achieve. How far away from that life do you live?

"LIFE IS OVER, START LIVING."

It is not about death—it is about the transition to death. We all know it's coming and that we're moving towards it. Accept the finality and know that it is not the end. Know that time is of the essence, and now is all we have. If now is not the right time, when is it going to be right? See it as fuel, not as punishment.

"The most happy man is he who knows how to bring into relation the end and beginning of his life."
—JOHANN WOLFGANG VON GOETHE, GERMAN POET

There are no do-overs. Live life in your greatest vision. Live to your greatest dream. Live with the fullest mindset and you'll be the most joyous person on earth.

"I would rather die of passion than of boredom."
—EMILE ZOLA, FRENCH NOVELIST

Bottom Line for Wisdom is the Beginning: I believe that death is a part of life. I choose to not focus on the sadness of losing another loved one, or my time being done. Let's focus on the now, the relationships in our space, have conversations that matter, and spend time with people who are important …. I'm going to fill the time I have with things that matter to me.

"Death may be the greatest of all human blessings."
—SOCRATES, GREEK PHILOSOPHER

Wisdom is the Beginning Personal Activity: We've all lost someone special to us; it is sad and depressing. Believing they are looking down on you today, what kind of life would they want to see you leading? Would they want you to be sad that they are gone? Yes! Would they want you to live the rest of your life in sadness? Not likely.

Would they want you to move on and live to your fullest? I believe they would.

Conclusion

I know exactly where the idea for this book started. As a young boy I loved going to spend time at the family business, not any typical family business, but a personal growth seminar. There was a seminar for adults, then during the summer my mom and grandmother would hold programs for teens. I didn't know there was any other way to spend part of a summer!

As I grew older and spent more time at the adult program (while continuing my involvement with the summer programs), I realized that the same problems and issues were discussed in each program. Additionally, people would admit that they committed the same errors in judgment over and over, never seeming to learn the error in their ways.

I specifically asked my family once as to why people conducted their lives in ways that were not healthy or brought them closer to their goal. From my young point of view, everyone had grown up with the same ideas, thoughts and lessons as I had in my family.

Gregory B. Davis

They explained to me that not everyone had the same set of knowledge in the world and some had different family knowledge and lessons learned. I understand this now and want as many people as possible to have the life lessons others posssess to make more out of their lives.

The key to a successful life, and the goal of this book, are to encourage you to learn from others before life's challenges are encountered. Consider another point of view when facing one difficult circumstance improve your mindset on how you think about what you face.

The challenges make us who we are; you can see that and learn from them and others now, or you can learn it later in life. Who you are and how you face roadblocks and difficult circumstances will have great bearing on the enjoyment and extent you live your life.

When all else fails, reread this book and do something different. When you change your approach and face conflict in a different frame of mind, there will be a new outcome. Simply moving your position will pay dividends.

When I find myself in a situation and things are not working out for me (and I become frustrated), the question I turn to is: "What can I do differently in this situation to obtain what I want?"

As people age, they tend to believe they have more and more of the answers and become more rigid. At the same time, the problems we face as we age become more complex and the manners in which we solved past issues don't always prove successful. This is a dangerous combination for big dilemmas or disputes becoming detrimental to an individual or couple. In life, the person with the most flexibility, knowledge and openness comes out ahead.

> "The greatest discovery of my generation is that a human being can alter his life by altering his attitudes."
> —WILLIAM JAMES, AMERICAN PHILOSOPHER

You may have approached the dilemma on numerous occasions and still no resolution has been found. Now you have new information, a new insight to solve problems. You might have passed up the opportunity one or a thousand times. However, now is the time to take the chance and move forward. There is never a wrong time to do the right thing.

> "To find yourself, think for yourself."
> —ATTICUS, ANCIENT PHILOSOPHER

When you find yourself, you'll find your truth. The most powerful state of being in the world is being secure about who you are, and what you know and don't know about yourself, and life. Once you admit you don't know everything about the situation, individual, yourself, life, and the future, you'll be on to explore and encounter newness.

Closed mindedness is one of the biggest hurdles you'll deal with, and on the other side is open mindedness which will open you to a bigger world. Not wanting to learn will bring you the lesson until you (painfully) grasp it. Wisdom is the beginning of opening your mind and life to a bigger world.

"Is there anyone so wise as to learn by the experience of others?"
—Voltaire, French writer

Yes, you are! That is an incredible part of reading this book and learning. My belief is that your life will be impacted by reading this book, you've gained new knowledge. While we are all in this life together, we must each individually find our own way. Take what you can from this book and live your best life. You deserve to have the life you've always dreamed.

Bottom Line for Wisdom is the Beginning: By reading this book, I believe you've learned and that you're committed to making your life better. Now that you have increased knowledge to make it happen and you're ahead in the game , put the knowledge into action and create the life you've always wanted and have been working towards. Your payoff is living in passion with dreams coming true.

I want to hear about your success with the changes and insights you've made in your life after reading *Wisdom is the Beginning*.

Preview of my upcoming book
Coming in Spring 2021

Life Unspoken

The more you share, the closer you come to true relationships

Introduction

When you think about your life and analyze the things that really matter to you— the ones that move you forward, and keep you feeling loved and alive— those are, without a doubt, your meaningful relationships.

You encounter love and meaning when you connect with others in a deep manner, by choosing to be vulnerable. It is important to note that what you verbally and emotionally put into each relationship is what you'll receive in return; the amount you are open, and allow others to see your inner self, will lead to the amount others will open with you. Because only when you embrace community will community embrace you, and at this point you will experience connection, community, and belonging.

Part of what I do for a living is present a family and teen program called *Choices Teen and Family Camp*. I have unmistakably learned, over and over again, that our closest relationships are the center of our wellbeing as humans. So, what is keeping you from fully thriving in yours?

During one of the summers, I witnessed an interaction that has forever changed the way I feel and think about the presence of silence in my life, and today I would like to share that with you:

The teen and family summer program normally receives approximately 35 families who work on their growth as a family; it starts with the personal growth of the children and then as a family unit— noting that parents had previously worked on their own personal betterment before working on their relationship with their kids. The goal of this program is to improve that relationship, taking it to the next more-loving level. For this specific memory and exercise, I was in front of the room filled with approximately 120 individuals (parents and children), and I was taken aback by the power and insight of one child.

The activity we were working on required each family to come to the front of the room and respond to a series of questions. The children, with whom we had been working with and preparing for this interaction over the prior few days were given the first turn.

We started with this question: "What is one thing the parent could do something about to improve the relationship?"

The child standing in front of the parent said: "Don't lie to me and stay in silence about your life."

The parent was surprised to hear this and took a minute, trying to understand where the child was coming from with such a comment. Then the parent, with complete focus and attention on the child, responded: "I do not lie to you, I'm very open with you about my life. What is the reason you'd ask that from me?"

The child quickly said: "When you get home every evening and I ask how your day went, you always respond "fine" then you go into your room in silence... and I know that doesn't mean fine. You are not fine."

The parent was emotionally disconcerted, but certainly owned up to the distance that this habit had created and what it communicated in their relationship.

It took me quite a few days to completely wrap my head around this profound family moment. So today, I ask you again, what is keeping you from fully thriving in your closest relationships? I learned that one of the most significant reasons is this: silence.

I am a son, a husband, a father, a brother, a friend. Since that family camp, I have taken the lessons from this story for myself and all the relationships in my life.

Wildly interesting is that when an individual turns to the game of silence in their relationships, the internal voices within both parties are **anything but silent.** When this environment is created—in any type of relationship—

there is lack of information, expression and conversation on both sides. Both individuals turn inwards on themselves, deepening their internal voices into a **dark place tucked away** in their thoughts. Next, unfortunately, a lot of mind reading begins, and what they are really left with is the hurtful questioning about the other's commitment to the relationship, **the space, and silence between them**. In many cases, the relationship has no chance to grow, learn, or even reach a common ground as the other individual is static with only themself to take the relationship somewhere, somehow.

Therefore, I ask you; does **silence** make you happy? No. It is **love** that makes you happy. It is **connection** that keeps you in a good place. It is belonging... and it all starts with **you saying the words.**

I acknowledge that opening can be a frightening endeavor and this very fear can set up decisions which impact our entire lives and relationships. We all have faced rejection and disappointment at some point in our life, and when our moment of vulnerability was rejected or not returned, it hurt. In a way, it might seem safer to keep quiet and closed off, versus being open to others.

While in the short term, **unspoken words** have the desired effect of making you feel safe, over the long term, secrets lead to more secrets and the subsequent lack of ability to **understand what should be kept to oneself, and what is healing to say.** Added up, all of these factors (secrets, silence, and loneliness) are impacting our health in a dramatic manner.

Today, right at this moment, the silence in your life might be defining your closest relationships and expanding your loneliness. All this in the belief that you're creating a perceived self-preservation, but the truth is that people in your life see it and feel it.

So, I would like you to ask yourself this: What do I want out of my life? Am I happy with my current relationships? Am I fulfilled, living at peace and experiencing belonging to my community?

To me, it seems worth reconsidering your choice of silence. In this book, together we will examine how and why silence is used in our relationships; we will see the value and benefits of sharing secrets, unveil the reasons to open up, and learn the steps that will bring us healing.

Shall we begin?

Endnotes

Box & Davis Family Quotes

Failure

- Keep failure out of your heart. - Gregory B. Davis
- Just because I fail doesn't mean I'm a failure. - Gregory B. Davis

Fear

- Step out in your faith and fear. - Thelma Box
- Part of what I fear I create in my life. - Gregory B. Davis
- Your greatest fears are meant to be shared. - Gregory B. Davis
- To live life to the fullest, you must lose the attachment to your fears. - Gregory B. Davis

Unhappiness: Happy vs. Unhappy

- Happiness must start on the inside. - Gregory B. Davis
- There is no end state of a perfect life, only the experience through life. - Gregory B. Davis

Change

- Change from any point of view is not good or bad. It is simply an uncomfortable part of life. - Gregory B. Davis
- Change begins in the mind and happens from the inside out. - Gregory B. Davis
- Change is up to you. - Thelma Box

Relationship

- Just because we disagree in no way does it mean I'm rejecting you. - Gregory B. Davis
- Needy people are demanding people. - Gregory B. Davis
- The person you married 10, 15, 40 years ago is no longer here. - Mary & Joe Davis
- Your loved ones can do nothing with nothing. - Gregory B. Davis

Relationship: I Can Change Him/Her

- You don't have to agree with them but you do have to live with them. - Gregory B. Davis
- You cannot get the time back you wasted fussing and fighting. - Gregory B. Davis
- You can only change you. - Gregory B. Davis
- In order for others to feel safe, you must create a safe environment. - Gregory B. Davis
- You can love through imperfections. - Gregory B. Davis

Relationship: My Partner Should Agree with Me

- Disagreement does NOT equal rejection. - Gregory B. Davis
- What are you really fighting about in your relationship? - Mary & Joe Davis
- Those who believe that absolute agreement equals true love has never been and never will be in love. - Gregory B. Davis

Relationship: Everyone Should Like Me

- Life is not about being liked; it is about being loved and respected. - Gregory B. Davis

Relationship: People Will Let You Down

- When you are attached to the outcome of other's actions you will be disappointed. - Gregory B. Davis
- Get out of your judgments and live life. - Gregory B. Davis
- Only Judge yourself versus yourself as you were yesterday. - Gregory B. Davis

Relationship: Addictions

- The secret is there are no secrets. - Gregory B. Davis
- Chemicals are not your friend. - Gregory B. Davis
- Addictions don't make you happy they just mask what makes you sad. - Gregory B. Davis
- Forgiveness is a decision; it may need to be made more than once. - Gregory B. Davis

Rejection

- See rejection as a start of new possibilities. - Gregory B. Davis
- Rejection says more about them than me. - Gregory B. Davis

Self-Limiting: No Time

- The opposite of success isn't failure, it is an excuse. - Gregory B. Davis

- We already have all the time there is - use it wisely. - Gregory B. Davis
- Don't let time get in the way with your relationships with people. - Gregory B. Davis

Self-Limiting: Not Enough X

- What are you costing yourself by not giving 100 percent. - Gregory B. Davis

Self-Limiting: Life Out of Balance

- Do just one thing at a time. - Gregory B. Davis

Self-Limiting: Waiting for Life to Happen

- Wishing it, wanting it and doing it are very different things. - Gregory B. Davis
- Are you here to give it your all or just watch? - Gregory B. Davis

Self-Limiting: Guilt

- Guilt is never positive. - Gregory B. Davis

Life is Inharmonic: Life should be fair

- There are times when we must deal with what is. - Gregory B. Davis

Life is Inharmonic: Being Alone

- Being alone is the best vitamin for the soul. - Gregory B. Davis
- The more we love ourselves, the easier it is to love others. - Mary & Joe Davis
- You are alone because you choose to feel that way. - Gregory B. Davis

Life is Inharmonic: Sadness

- Be emotionally honest with yourself. - Gregory B. Davis
- Your choice of a life time get better or not. - Gregory B. Davis
- You can't carry garbage around and smell like a rose. - Gregory B. Davis

Discouragement

- What we are now is not as important as what we may become. - Gregory B. Davis
- Even when discouraged, you are strong. - Gregory B. Davis

Death

- Life is over, start living. - Gregory B. Davis

All Quotes

Title Page

* Employ your time in improving yourself by other men's writings, so that you shall gain easily what others have labored hard for. - Socrates, Greek philosopher[6]

Who am I?

* True life is lived when tiny changes occur. - Leo Tolstoy, Russian writer [7]

Introduction

* We come altogether fresh and raw into several stages of life, and often find ourselves without experience, despite our years. - Francois de la Rochefoucauld, French writer and memoirist[8]

---

6   Socrates, "see quote above," accessed June, 2020, https://www.brainyquote.com/quotes/socrates_122574.

7   Tolstoy, "see quote above," accessed June, 2020, https://www.countryliving.com/life/entertainment/g5153/positive-quotes-about-change/.

8   Rochefoucauld, "see quote above," accessed June 2020, https://quotefancy.com/quote/1387812/Fran-ois-de-La-Rochefoucauld-We-come-altogether-fresh-and-raw-into-the-several-stages-of.

- Self-knowledge comes from knowing other men. - Johann Wolfgang von Goethe, German poet[9]

Opening Story

- It would...be a beautiful thing, to pass through life together hypnotized in our dreams: your dream for your country, our dream for humanity; our dream for science. - Pierre Curie, Nobel Prize winner[10]

Wisdom is the Beginning

- Man arrives as a novice at each age of his life. - Nicolas Chamfort, French writer[11]
- Appreciation is a wonderful thing: It makes what is excellent in others belong to us as well. - Voltaire, French writer[12]
- We are more interested in making others believe we are happy than in trying to be happy ourselves. - Francois de la Rochefoucauld, French writer and memoirist[13]

---

9   von Goethe, "see quote above," accessed June, 2020, http://greatestquotes.net/73/self-knowledge-comes-from-knowing-other-men-johann-wolfgang-von-goethe.html.

10   Des Jardins, Julie. "Madame Curie's Passion". Smithsonian Magazine. Accessed June 2020. www.smithsonianmag.com/history/madame-curies-passion-74183598/.

11   Chamfort, "see quote above," accessed June, 2020, https://www.quotetab.com/quote/by-nicolas-chamfort/man-arrives-as-a-novice-at-each-age-of-his-life.

12   Voltaire, "see quote above," accessed June, 2020, http://quodid.com/quotes/11704/voltaire/appreciation-is-a-wonderful-thing-it-makes-what.

13   Rochefoucauld, "see quote above," accessed June 2020, https://www.quotetab.com/quote/by-francois-de-la-rochefoucauld/we-are-more-interested-in-

- Common sense is not so common. - Voltaire, French writer[14]
- What we achieve inwardly will change outer reality. - Plutarch, Greek philosopher [15]
- Learning never exhausts the mind. - Leonardo da Vinci, Italian artist, scientist and engineer[16]
- The unexamined life is not worth living. - Socrates, Greek philosopher[17]

Failure

- Do not fear mistakes. You will know failure. Continue to reach out. - Benjamin Franklin, founding father of US Declaration of Independence[18]
- My great concern is not whether you have failed, but whether you are content with your failure. - Abraham Lincoln, US President[19]

---

making-others-believe-we-are-happy-than-in-trying-to-be?source=make-others-happy.

14   Voltaire, "see quote above," accessed June, 2020, https://www.goodreads.com/quotes/3915-common-sense-is-not-so-common.

15   Plutarch, "see quote above," accessed June, 2020, https://www.brainyquote.com/quotes/plutarch_120365.

16   da Vinci, "see quote above," accessed June, 2020, https://www.lagazzettai-taliana.com/people/8450-learning-never-exhausts-the-mind-leonardo-da-vin-ci-1452-1519.

17   Socrates, "see quote above," accessed June, 2020, https://www.the-philoso-phy.com/unexamined-life-worth-living-socrates.

18   Franklin, "see quote above," accessed June, 2020, https://www.fearlessmo-tivation.com/2016/05/16/11-powerful-benjamin-franklin-quotes-leadership-suc-cess/.

19   Lincoln, "see quote above," accessed June, 2020, https://www.optimize.me/quotes/abraham-lincoln/21032-my-great-concern-is-not-whether-you-have/.

- Mistakes are the portals of discovery. - James Joyce, Irish novelist and poet[20]
- I've not failed. I've just found 10,000 ways that won't work. - Thomas Edison, US inventor, business man[21]
- Fall down seven times, get up eight. - Japanese quote[22]
- The doer alone learneth. - Friedrich Nietzsche, German philosopher[23]
- Every man is guilty of all the good he did not do. - Voltaire, French writer[24]
- Keep failure out of your heart. - Gregory B. Davis
- Just because I fail doesn't mean I'm a failure. - Gregory B. Davis

Fear

- We promise according to our hopes and perform according to our fears. - Francois de la Rochefoucauld, French writer and memoirist[25]

---

20   Joyce, "see quote above," accessed June, 2020, https://www.passiton.com/inspirational-quotes/6462-mistakes-are-the-portals-of-discovery.

21   Edison, "see quote above," accessed June, 2020, https://www.goodreads.com/book/show/46085492-i-ve-not-failed-i-ve-just-found-10-000-ways-that-won-t-work.

22   Japanese Quote, "see quote above," accessed June, 2020, https://coolerinsights.com/2011/03/6-lessons-in-japanese-resilience/.

23   Nietzsche, "see quote above," accessed June, 2020, https://allauthor.com/quotes/160097/.

24   Voltaire, "see quote above," accessed June, 2020, https://philosiblog.com/2012/11/21/every-man-is-guilty-of-all-the-good-he-did-not-do/.

25   Rochefoucauld, "see quote above," accessed June 2020, http://quoteseed.com/quotes/francois-de-la-rochefoucauld/francois-de-la-rochefoucauld-we-promise-according-to-our-hopes-and/.

- **Step out in your faith and fear. - Thelma Box**
- Do the things you fear and the death of fear is certain. - Ralph Waldo Emerson, American writer[26]
- Fear is pain arising from the anticipation of evil. - Aristotle, Ancient Greek philosopher[27]
- It is a queer thing, but imaginary troubles are harder to bear than actual ones. - Dorothea Dix, 19th century American activist[28]
- We can easily forgive a child who is afraid of the dark; the real tragedy of life is when men are afraid of the light. - Plato, Greek philosopher[29]
- There are more things to alarm us than to harm us, and we suffer more often in **apprehension** than reality. - Lucius Annaeus Seneca (Seneca the Elder) [emphasis is mine][30]
- If you keep feeling a point that has been sharpened, the point cannot long preserve its sharpness. - Lao Tzu, Chinese philosopher[31]

---

26   Emerson, "see quote above," accessed June 2020, http://kevinkirkland.co/quote-collection/.

27   Aristotle, "see quote above," accessed June 2020, https://www.goodreads.com/quotes/62143-fear-is-pain-arising-from-the-anticipation-of-evil.

28   Dix, "see quote above," accessed June 2020, https://quotefancy.com/quote/1165175/Dorothy-Dix-It-is-a-queer-thing-but-imaginary-troubles-are-har-der-to-bear-than-actual#:~:text=Dorothy%20Dix%20Quote%3A%20%E2%80%-9CIt%20is,%E2%80%9D%20(7%20wallpapers)%20%2D%20Quotefancy.

29   Plato, "see quote above," accessed June 2020, https://www.goodreads.com/quotes/19198-we-can-easily-forgive-a-child-who-is-afraid-of.

30   Seneca, "see quote above," accessed June 2020, https://www.quotetab.com/quotes/by-lucius-annaeus-seneca.

31   Lao Tzu, "see quote above," accessed June 2020, https://www.yellowbridge.com/onlinelit/daodejing09.php.

- Death is not the worst that can happen to men. - Plato, Greek philosopher[32]
- Everything you've ever wanted is on the other side of fear. - George Addair, real-estate developer in post–Civil War Atlanta[33]
- Life is to be entered upon with courage. - Alexis de Tocqueville, French aristocrat, diplomat, political scientist and historian[34]
- The pleasures of love are always in proportion to our fears. - Stendhal, French author[35]
- **Part of what I fear I create in my life. - Gregory B. Davis**
- **Your greatest fears are meant to be shared. - Gregory B. Davis**
- **To live life to the fullest, you must lose the attachment to your fears. - Gregory B. Davis**
- How very little can be done under the spirit of fear. - Florence Nightingale, pioneer of modern nursing[36]

---

32   Plato, "see quote above," accessed June 2020, https://www.barnesandnoble.com/w/plato-parmenides-plato/1128029890.

33   Addair, "see quote above," accessed June 2020, https://www.georgeaddair.com/.

34   Tocqueville, "see quote above," accessed June 2020, https://www.staugustine.net/blogs/rectify-names-a-blog-on-publishing/e2809clife-is-to-be-entered-upon-with-couragee2809d-march-4-2013/.

35   Stendhal, "see quote above," accessed June 2020, http://quodid.com/quotes/10606/stendhal/the-pleasures-of-love-are-always-in-proportion.

36   Nightingale, "see quote above," accessed June 2020, https://www.cufi.org.uk/spotlight/how-very-little-can-be-done-under-the-spirit-of-fear-florence-nightingales-amazing-legacy-is-a-lesson-for-today/.

Unhappiness: Happy vs. Unhappy

- **Happiness must start on the inside. - Gregory B. Davis**
- Happiness is a state of activity. - Aristotle, Ancient Greek philosopher[37]
- The only joy in the world is to begin. - Cesare Pavese, Italian poet[38]
- Happiness is not something ready made. It comes from your own actions. - Dalai Lama, spiritual leader[39]
  We tend to forget that happiness doesn't come as a result of getting something we don't have, but rather of recognizing and appreciating what we do have. - Friedrich Keonig, German inventor[40]
- **There is no end state of a perfect life, only the experience through life. - Gregory B. Davis**
- Very little is needed to make a happy life; it is all within yourself, in your way of thinking. - Marcus Aurelius Antoninus, Roman emperor and philosopher[41]
- Before we set our hearts too much upon anything, let us examine how happy they are who already possess

---

37   Aristotle, "see quote above," accessed June 2020, https://link.springer.com/article/10.1007/s11518-018-5383-7.

38   Pavese, "see quote above," accessed June 2020, http://www.notable-quotes.com/p/pavese_cesare.html.

39   Dalai Lama, "see quote above," accessed June 2020, https://www.brainy-quote.com/quotes/dalai_lama_166116.

40   Keonig, "see quote above," accessed June 2020, https://www.treasurequo-tes.com/quotes/we-tend-to-forget-that-happiness-doesnt-come-2.

41   Antoninus, "see quote above," accessed June 2020, http://www.inspiration.rightattitudes.com/authors/marcus-aurelius-antoninus-augustus/.

it. - Francois de la Rochefoucauld, French writer and memoirist [42]
- We never live; we are always in the expectation of living. - Voltaire, French writer[43]
- Happiness depends upon ourselves. - Aristotle, Ancient Greek philosopher[44]

Problems

- Every man has his secret sorrows which the world knows not; and often times we call a man cold when he is only sad. - Henry Wadsworth Longfellow, American poet[45]
- Life is not a problem to be solved, but a reality to be experienced. - Soren Kierkegaard, Danish philosopher [46]
- Running away from a problem only increases the distance from the solution. - Anonymous[47]
- If you can solve your problem, then what is the need of worrying? If you cannot solve it, then what is the use of

---

42 Rochefoucauld, "see quote above," accessed June 2020, https://quotefancy. com/quote/1386905/Fran-ois-de-La-Rochefoucauld-Before-we-set-our-hearts-too-much-upon-anything-let-us.

43 Voltaire, "see quote above," accessed June 2020, https://www.optimize.me/ quotes/voltaire/20279-we-never-live-we-are-always-in-the-expe/.

44 Aristotle, "see quote above," accessed June 2020, https://www.goodreads. com/quotes/1150-happiness-depends-upon-ourselves.

45 Longfellow, "see quote above," accessed June 2020, https://www.good-newsnetwork.org/longfellow-quote-on-sadness/.

46 Kiekegaard, "see quote above," accessed June 2020, https://www.alexrovi-ra.com/en/soluciones/articulo/soren-kierkegaard.

47 Anonymous, "see quote above," accessed June 2020, https://www.entrepre-neur.com/article/288957.

worrying? - Shantideva, 8th-century Indian Buddhist scholar[48]

- Giving up is the most painful way of solving a problem. - Anonymous[49]

- No problem can withstand the assault of sustained thinking. - Voltaire, French writer[50]

- Bad times have scientific value. These are occasions a good learner would not miss. - Ralph Waldo Emerson, American writer[51]

- The gem cannot be polished without friction, nor man perfected without trials. - Chinese Proverb[52]

Change

- **Change from any point of view is not good or bad. It is simply an uncomfortable part of life. - Gregory B. Davis**

- All things are only transitory. - Johann Wolfgang von Goethe, German poet[53]

---

48   Shantideva, "see quote above," accessed June 2020, https://www.beliefnet.com/quotes/health/s/shantideva/if-you-can-solve-your-problem-then-what-is-the-ne.aspx.

49   Anonymous, "see quote above," accessed June 2020, https://www.entrepreneur.com/article/288957.

50   Voltaire, "see quote above," accessed June 2020, https://quotationcelebration.wordpress.com/2018/05/11/no-problem-can-withstand-the-assault-of-sustained-thinking-voltaire/.

51   Emerson, "see quote above," accessed June 2020, https://wisdomquotes.com/ralph-waldo-emerson-quotes/.

52   Chinese Proverb, "see quote above," accessed June 2020, https://www.quotes.net/quote/9113.

53   von Goethe, "see quote above," accessed June 2020, https://quotes.yourdictionary.com/author/johann-wolfgang-von-goethe/613958.

- Things do not change; we change. - Henry David Thoreau, American Essayist[54]
- Everyone thinks of changing the world, but no one things of changing himself. - Leo Tolstoy. Russian novelist[55]
- The universe is change; our life is what our thoughts make it. - Marcus Aurelius, Roman leader[56]
- Change your opinions, keep to your principles; change your leaves, keep intact your roots. - Victor Hugo, French poet[57]
- Loss is nothing else but change, and change is Nature's delight. - Marcus Aurelius, Roman leader[58]
- Life belongs to the living, and he who lives must be prepared for changes.- Johann Wolfgang von Goethe, German poet[59]
- **Change begins in the mind and happens from the inside out. - Gregory B. Davis**
- If you want something you have never had, you must be willing to do something you have never done. -

54   Thoreau, "see quote above," accessed June 2020, http://quodid.com/quotes/6556/henry-david-thoreau/things-do-not-change-we-change.

55   Tolstoy, "see quote above," accessed June 2020, https://julesx.com/10-powerful-leadership-quotes/.

56   Aurelius, "see quote above," accessed June 2020, https://www.brainyquote.com/quotes/marcus_aurelius_383109.

57   Hugo, "see quote above," accessed June 2020, https://tinybuddha.com/wisdom-quotes/change-opinions-keep-principles-change-leaves-keep-intact-roots/.

58   Aurelius, "see quote above," accessed June 2020, https://www.brainyquote.com/quotes/marcus_aurelius_148748.

59   von Goethe, "see quote above," accessed June 2020,https://www.treasurequotes.com/quotes/life-belongs-to-the-living-and-he-who-lives-m.

Thomas Jefferson, Founding Father, Third President of the U.S.[60]

- **Change is up to you. - Thelma Box**
- The most faithful mirror is an old friend. - Atticus, Ancient philosopher[61]
- There is nothing permanent except change. - Heraclitus, Greek philosopher [62]

Relationship

- Weakness on both sides is, as we know, the motto of all quarrels. - Voltaire, French writer[63]
- **Just because we disagree in no way does it mean I'm rejecting you. - Gregory B. Davis**
- If you wish to be loved, love. - Hecato, Greek stoic philosopher[64]
- **Needy people are demanding people. - Gregory B. Davis**
- **The person you married 10, 15, 40 years ago is no longer here. - Mary & Joe Davis**

---

60   Jefferson, "see quote above," accessed June 2020, https://www.monticello. org/site/research-and-collections/if-you-want-something-you-have-never-had-spurious-quotation.

61   Atticus, "see quote above," accessed June 2020, https://www.goodreads. com/quotes/7077035-the-most-faithful-mirror-is-an-old-friend.

62   Heraclitus, "see quote above," accessed June 2020, https://www.brainyquo-te.com/quotes/heraclitus_165537.

63   Voltaire, "see quote above," accessed June 2020, https://www.brainyquote. com/quotes/voltaire_164909#:~:text=Voltaire%20Quotes&text=Weakness%20 on%20both%20sides%20is%2C%20as%20we%20know,the%20motto%20of%20 all%20quarrels..

64   Hecato, "see quote above," accessed June 2020, https://www.goodreads. com/quotes/820171-if-you-wish-to-be-loved-love.

- Marriage is three parts love and seven parts forgiveness of sins. - Laozi, Chinese philosopher[65]
- **Your loved ones can do nothing with nothing. - Gregory B. Davis**

Relationship: I Can Change Him/Her

- **You don't have to agree with them but you do have to live with them. - Gregory B. Davis**
- We are all full of weakness and errors; let us mutually pardon each other our follies - it is the first law of nature. - Voltaire, French writer[66]
- It is not the lack of love, but a lack of friendship, that makes unhappy marriages. Friedrich Nietzsche, German philosopher[67]
- **You cannot get the time back you wasted fussing and fighting. - Gregory B. Davis**
- **You can only change you. - Gregory B. Davis**
- In order for others to feel safe, you must create a safe environment. - Gregory B. Davis
- **You can love through imperfections. - Gregory B. Davis**

---

65   Laozi, "see quote above," accessed June 2020, https://www.quotetab.com/quote/by-lao-tzu/marriage-is-three-parts-love-and-seven-parts-forgiveness-of-sins.
66   Voltaire, "see quote above," accessed June 2020, https://www.quotes.net/quote/74009.
67   Nietzsche, "see quote above," accessed June 2020, https://www.quotedb.com/quotes/3274.

Relationship: My Partner Should Agree with Me

- **Disagreement does NOT equal rejection. - Gregory B. Davis**
- Victor and vanquished never unite in substantial agreement. -Tacitus, Roman historian[68]
- A bad peace is worse than war. - Tacitus, Roman historian[69]
- The ear is the avenue to the heart. - Voltaire, French writer[70]
- We often refuse to accept an idea merely because the tone of voice in which it has been expressed is unsympathetic to us. - Friedrich Nietzsche, German philosopher[71]
- We cannot wish for that we know not. - Voltaire, French writer[72]

---

68   Tacitus, "see quote above," accessed June 2020, https://www.brainyquote. com/quotes/tacitus_117945.

69   Tacitus, "see quote above," accessed June 2020, https://www.goodreads. com/quotes/543400-a-bad-peace-is-worse-than-war#:~:text=Quote%20by%20 Tacitus%3A%20%E2%80%9CA%20bad,peace%20is%20worse%20than%20 war.%E2%80%9D.

70   Voltaire, "see quote above," accessed June 2020, https://www.brainyquote. com/quotes/voltaire_145545#:~:text=Voltaire%20%2D%20The%20ear%20is%20 the%20avenue%20to%20the%20heart..

71   Nietzsche, "see quote above," accessed June 2020, https://www.brainyquo- te.com/quotes/friedrich_nietzsche_390523#:~:text=Friedrich%20Nietzsche%20 Quotes&text=We%20often%20refuse%20to%20accept%20an%20idea%20mere- ly%20because%20the,expressed%20is%20unsympathetic%20to%20us..

72   Voltaire, "see quote above," accessed June 2020, https://www.allgreatquo- tes.com/quote-469321/.

- **What are you really fighting about in your relationship? - Mary & Joe Davis**
- **Those who believe that absolute agreement equals true love has never been and never will be in love. - Gregory B. Davis**

Relationship: Everyone Should Like Me

- Love is no assignment of cowards. - Ovid, Roman poet [73]
- *Life is not about being liked; it is about being loved and respected. - Gregory B. Davis*
- If we have not peace within ourselves, it is in vain to seek it from outward sources. - Francois de la Rochefoucauld, French writer and memoirist[74]

Relationship: People Will Let You Down

- **When you are attached to the outcome of other's actions you will be disappointed. - Gregory B. Davis**
- We are all strong enough to bear other men's misfortunes. - Francois de la Rochefoucauld, French writer and memoirist[75]

---

73   Ovid, "see quote above," accessed June 2020, https://spiritualityhealth.com/quotes/ovid-on-the-bravery-required-for-love.
74   Rochefoucauld, "see quote above," accessed June 2020, https://www.forbes.com/quotes/3017/.
75   Rochefoucauld, "see quote above," accessed June 2020, https://www.brainyquote.com/quotes/francois_de_la_rochefouca_400370.

- Get out of your judgments and live life. - Gregory B. Davis
- Only Judge yourself versus yourself as you were yesterday. - Gregory B. Davis

Relationship: Addictions

- **The secret is there are no secrets. - Gregory B. Davis**
- We do not despise all those who have vices, but we do despise those that have no virtue. - Francois de la Rochefoucauld, French writer and memoirist[76]
- **Chemicals are not your friend. - Gregory B. Davis**
- I found the perfect addiction - workaholic - it is so socially acceptable. - Unknown[77]
- **Addictions don't make you happy they just mask what makes you sad. - Gregory B. Davis**
- **Forgiveness is a decision; it may need to be made more than once. - Gregory B. Davis**
- Holding on to anger is like grasping a hot coal with the intent of throwing it at someone else; you are the one who gets burned. - Buddha, Philosopher[78]

---

76   Rochefoucauld, "see quote above," accessed June 2020, https://www.quotetab.com/quote/by-francois-de-la-rochefoucauld/we-do-not-despise-all-those-who-have-vices-but-we-do-despise-those-that-have-no?source=vices.
77   Unknown
78   Buddha, "see quote above," accessed June 2020, https://www.brainyquote.com/quotes/buddha_104025

Rejection

- There is nothing good or bad, but thinking makes it so. - Shakespeare, playwright[79]
- **See rejection as a start of new possibilities. - Gregory B. Davis**
- **Rejection says more about them than me. - Gregory B. Davis**
- Our greatest glory is not in never falling, but rising every time we fall. - Confucius, Chinese Philosopher[80]

Self-Limiting

- There is nothing in the world more shameful than establishing one's self on lies and fables. - Johann Wolfgang von Goethe, German poet[81]
- The greater part of our happiness or misery depends upon our dispositions, and not upon our circumstance. - Martha Washington, wife of George Washington, First President of the United States[82]

---

79   Shakespeare, "see quote above," accessed June 2020, http://www.quotationspage.com/quote/41245.html.

80   Confucius, "see quote above," accessed June 2020, http://www.quotethee.com/our-greatest-glory-is-not-in-never-falling-but-rising-every-time-we-fall-confucius-600x600oc-ig-lucentquotes/.

81   von Goethe, "see quote above," accessed June 2020, https://quotefancy.com/quote/839539/Johann-Wolfgang-von-Goethe-There-is-nothing-in-the-world-more-shameful-than-establishing.

82   Washington, "see quote above," accessed June 2020, https://www.goodreads.com/topic/show/349838-favorite-quotes---thread-1.

- I attribute my success to this: I never gave or took any excuse. - Florence Nightingale, pioneer of modern nursing[83]
- It is man's own mind, not his enemy or foe, that lures him to evil ways. - Buddha, Philosopher[84]
- If one speaks or acts with a pure mind, happiness follows him like a shadow that never leaves him - Buddha scripts, Dhammapada Verse 2[85]
- He who does not think much of himself is much more esteemed than he imagines. - Johann Wolfgang von Goethe, German poet[86]

Self-Limiting: No Time

- One always has time enough, if one will apply it well. - Johann Wolfgang von Goethe, German poet[87]
- **The opposite of success isn't failure, it is an excuse. - Gregory B. Davis**
- Procrastination is the thief of time. Collar him! - Charles Dickens, English writer[88]

---

83   Nightingale, "see quote above," accessed June 2020, https://quoteinvestigator.com/2016/07/30/excuse/.

84   Buddha, "see quote above," accessed June 2020, https://jnanagni.wordpress.com/quotes/buddha/.

85   Buddha scripts, "see quote above," accessed June 2020, https://www.tipitaka.net/tipitaka/dhp/verseload.php?verse=002.

86   von Goethe, "see quote above," accessed June 2020, https://www.azquotes.com/quote/656267.

87   von Goethe, "see quote above," accessed June 2020, https://www.brainyquote.com/quotes/johann_wolfgang_von_goeth_118709.

88   Dickens, "see quote above," accessed June 2020, https://www.goodreads.

- He that is good for making excuses is seldom good for anything else. - Benjamin Franklin, founding father of US Declaration of Independence[89]
- An excuse is worse and more terrible than a lie; for an excuse is a lie guarded. - Alexander Pope, English poet[90]
- **We already have all the time there is - use it wisely. - Gregory B. Davis**
- Our life is frittered away by detail. Simplify, simplify. - Henry David Thoreau, American Essayist[91]
- **Don't let time get in the way with your relationships with people. - Gregory B. Davis**
- Hardly any human being is capable of pursuing two professions or two arts rightly. -Plato, Greek philosopher[92]
- Be happy for this moment. This moment is your life. - Omar Khayyam, Persian mathematician[93]
- Any excuse will serve a tyrant. - Aesop, Greek fabulist[94]

---

com/quotes/15368-procrastination-is-the-thief-of-time-collar-him.

89   Franklin, "see quote above," accessed June 2020, https://www.brainyquote.com/quotes/benjamin_franklin_383794.

90   Pope, "see quote above," accessed June 2020, http://quoteseed.com/quotes/alexander-pope/alexander-pope-an-excuse-is-worse-and-more-terrible/#:~:text=%E2%80%9CAn%20excuse%20is%20worse%20and,lie%20guarded.%E2%80%9D%20%E2%80%93%20Alexander%20Pope.

91   Thoreau, "see quote above," accessed June 2020, http://xenon.stanford.edu/~rfoon/files/quotes/files/thoreau.html.

92   Plato, "see quote above," accessed June 2020, http://immortalquotes.com/profile/platon.

93   Khayyam, "see quote above," accessed June 2020, https://www.brainyquote.com/quotes/omar_khayyam_378553

94   Aesop, "see quote above," accessed June 2020, https://www.brainyquote.

Self-Limiting: I'm Tired

- Life is one long process of getting tired. - Samuel Butler, the Younger, novelist, satirist, scholar[95]
- Life is too short, and the time we waste in yawning never can be regained. - Stendhal, French author, professor[96]
- Life is largely a matter of expectation. - Horace, author (version of Homer teaching)[97]
- Either do not attempt at all, or go through with it. - Ovid, Roman poet[98]

Self-Limiting: Not Enough X

- A useless life is an early death. - Johann Wolfgang von Goethe, German poet[99]
- Be content with what you have; rejoice in the way things are. When you realize there is nothing lacking,

com/quotes/aesop_136674.

95   Butler, "see quote above," accessed June 2020, http://quoteseed.com/quo-tes/samuel-butler/samuel-butler-life-is-one-long-process-of-getting/.

96   Stendhal, "see quote above," accessed June 2020, https://www.quotetab. com/quote/by-stendhal/life-is-too-short-and-the-time-we-waste-in-yawning-ne-ver-can-be-regained.

97   Horace, "see quote above," accessed June 2020, https://www.brainyquote. com/quotes/horace_152468#:~:text=Horace%20Quotes&text=Life%20is%20lar-gely%20a%20matter%20of%20expectation.,-Horace.

98   Ovid, "see quote above," accessed June 2020, https://www.forbes.com/ quotes/7284/.

99   von Goethe, "see quote above," accessed June 2020, https://www.goo-dreads.com/quotes/741838-a-useless-life-is-an-early-death.

the whole world belongs to you. - Lao Tzu, Chinese philosopher[100]

- Man is made by his belief. As he believes, so he is. - Bhagavad Gita, Hindu scripture[101]
- We forge the chains we wear in life. - Charles Dickens, English writer[102]
- Reflect upon your present blessings—of which every man has many not on your past misfortunes, of which all men have some. - Charles Dickens, English writer[103]
- He who lives in harmony with himself lives in harmony with the universe. - Marcus Aurelius, Roman leader[104]
- **What are you costing yourself by not giving 100 percent. - Gregory B. Davis**
- Why are you so enchanted by this world, when a mine of gold lies within you? - Rumi, Persian poet[105]
- Think not so much of what you lack as of what you have: but of the things that you have, select the best, and then reflect on how eagerly you would have sought

100   Lao Tzu, "see quote above," accessed June 2020, https://www.brainyquote.com/quotes/lao_tzu_393061.

101   Gita, "see quote above," accessed June 2020, https://www.goodreads.com/quotes/7574034-man-is-made-by-his-belief-as-he-believes-so.

102   Dickens, "see quote above," accessed June 2020, https://www.brainyquote.com/quotes/charles_dickens_379740.

103   Dickens, "see quote above," accessed June 2020, https://www.brainyquote.com/quotes/charles_dickens_121978.

104   Aurelius, "see quote above," accessed June 2020, https://www.brainyquote.com/quotes/marcus_aurelius_384175.

105   Rumi, "see quote above," accessed June 2020, https://quotefancy.com/quote/904052/Rumi-Why-are-you-so-enchanted-by-this-world-when-a-mine-of-gold-lies-within-you.

them if you did not have them. - Marcus Aurelius, Roman leader, Meditations[106]

Self-Limiting: Life Out of Balance

- There is nothing so terrible as activity without insight. - Johann Wolfgang von Goethe, German poet[107]
- God gave us the gift of life; it is up to us to give ourselves the gift of living well. - Voltaire, French writer[108]
- If you do not change direction, you may end up where you are heading. - Lao Tzu, Chinese philosopher[109]
- Beware the barrenness of a busy life. - Socrates, Greek philosopher[110]
- It is not enough to be busy. So are the ants. The question is: What are you busy about? - Henry David Thoreau, American Essayist[111]
- **Do just one thing at a time. - Gregory B. Davis**
- What lies behind you, and what lies in front of you,

106   Aurelius, "see quote above," accessed June 2020, https://www.goodreads.com/author/quotes/17212.Marcus_Aurelius?page=12.

107   von Goethe, "see quote above," accessed June 2020, https://www.brainyquote.com/quotes/johann_wolfgang_von_goeth_382514.

108   Voltaire, "see quote above," accessed June 2020, https://www.brainyquote.com/quotes/voltaire_134077.

109   Lao Tzu, "see quote above," accessed June 2020, https://beyondquarterlife.com/change-direction-may-end/.

110   Socrates, "see quote above," accessed June 2020, https://www.brainyquote.com/quotes/socrates_133712.

111   Thoreau, "see quote above," accessed June 2020, https://www.forbes.com/quotes/3974/.

pales in comparison to what lies inside you. - Ralph Waldo Emerson, American writer[112]

Self-Limiting: Waiting for Life to Happen

- Everybody wants to be somebody; nobody wants to grow. - Johann Wolfgang von Goethe, German poet[113]
- To see things in the seed, that is genius. - Lao Tzu, Chinese philosopher[114]
- If we are facing in the right direction, all we have to do is keep on walking. - Buddhist proverb[115]
- The secret of getting ahead is getting started. - Mark Twain, American writer[116]
- **Wishing it, wanting it and doing it are very different things. - Gregory B. Davis**
- The bold adventurer succeeds the best. - Ovid, Roman poet[117]

---

112   Emerson, "see quote above," accessed June 2020, https://www.brainyquote.com/quotes/ralph_waldo_emerson_386697.

113   von Goethe, "see quote above," accessed June 2020, http://www.quotationspage.com/quote/4395.html.

114   Lao Tzu, "see quote above," accessed June 2020, https://www.brainyquote.com/quotes/lao_tzu_103462.

115   Buddhist Proverb, "see quote above," accessed June 2020, https://tinybuddha.com/wisdom-quotes/if-we-are-facing-in-the-right-direction-all-we-have-to-do-is-keep-on-walking/#:~:text=If%20we%20are%20facing%20in,%2D%20Tiny%20Buddha

116   Twain, "see quote above," accessed June 2020, https://quotationcelebration.wordpress.com/2018/01/22/the-secret-of-getting-ahead-is-getting-started-mark-twain/.

117   Ovid, "see quote above," accessed June 2020, https://quotefancy.com/

- **Are you here to give it your all or just watch? - Gregory B. Davis**
- The only person you are destined to become is the person you decide to be. - Ralph Waldo Emerson, American writer[118]

Self-Limiting: Guilt

- No amount of guilt will change the past... - Umar ibn Al-Khattab, historical figure[119]
- One minute of patience, ten years of peace. - Greek proverb[120]
- When the past calls, let it go to voice mail. Believe me, it has nothing new to say. - Unknown
- Man is free at the moment he wishes to be. - Voltaire, French writer[121]
- **Guilt is never positive. - Gregory B. Davis**
- Certain defects are necessary for the existence of individuality. - Johann Wolfgang von Goethe, German poet [122]

---

quote/883309/Ovid-The-bold-adventurer-succeeds-the-best.

118   Emerson, "see quote above," accessed June 2020, https://www.goodreads.com/quotes/73656-the-only-person-you-are-destined-to-become-is-the.

119   Umar ibn Al-Khattab, "see quote above," accessed June 2020, https://www.goodreads.com/quotes/855080-no-amount-of-guilt-can-change-the-past-and-no.

120   Greek Proverb, "see quote above," accessed June 2020, https://www.goodreads.com/quotes/7392719-one-minute-of-patience-ten-years-of-peace

121   Voltaire, "see quote above," accessed June 2020, https://www.quotes.net/quote/6742.

122   von Goethe, "see quote above," accessed June 2020, https://www.brainyquote.com/quotes/johann_wolfgang_von_goeth_150534.

- Nothing is more wretched than the mind of a man conscious of guilt. - Plautus, Roman playwright[123]
- Where guilt is, rage and courage doth abound. - Ben Johnson, English playwright[124]
- He who lives without folly isn't so wise as he thinks. - Francois de la Rochefoucauld, French writer and memoirist[125]
- Next to the dog, the wastebasket is man's best friend. - Anonymous[126]
- Life is thickly sown with thorns, and I know no other remedy than to pass quickly through them. The longer we dwell on our misfortunes, the greater is their power to harm us. - Voltaire, French writer[127]

Life is Inharmonic

- Each player must accept the cards life deals him or her: but once they are in hand, he or she alone must

---

123   Plautus, "see quote above," accessed June 2020, https://www.quotes.net/quote/21017.

124   Johnson, "see quote above," accessed June 2020, https://www.azquotes.com/quote/558836#:~:text=Were%20Guilt%20is%2C%20Rage%20and%20Courage%20doth%20abound.,-Ben%20Jonson&text=%22Volpone%3B%20or%2C%20The%20fox,Bartholomew%20Fair..

125   Rochefoucauld, "see quote above," accessed June 2020, https://www.brainyquote.com/quotes/francois_de_la_rochefouca_403320#:~:text=Francois%20de%20La%20Rochefoucauld%20Quotes&text=He%20who%20lives%20without%20folly%20isn,so%20wise%20as%20he%20thinks.

126   Anonymous, "see quote above," accessed June 2020, https://www.forbes.com/quotes/562/.

127   Voltaire, "see quote above," accessed June 2020, https://wise-quote.com/Francois-Voltaire.

decide how to play the cards in order to win the game. - Voltaire, French writer[128]

- Our task is not to seek for love, but merely to seek and find all the barriers within yourself that you have built against it. - Rumi, Persian poet[129]

- Life is too short to be little. Man is never so manly as when he feels deeply, acts boldly, and expresses himself with frankness and with fervor. - Benjamin Disraeli, British statesman[130]

- Whatever you can do, or dream you can, begin it. Boldness has genius, power and magic in it. - attributed to Johann Wolfgang von Goethe, German poet[131]

Life is Inharmonic: Life should be fair

- We all have enough strength to endure the misfortune of others. - Francois de la Rochefoucauld, French writer and memoirist[132]

---

128   Voltaire, "see quote above," accessed June 2020, https://wise-quote.com/Francois-Voltaire
129   Rumi, "see quote above," accessed June 2020, https://mo-issa.com/2017/07/13-rumi-poems-to-awaken-the-love-within-us/.
130   Disraeli, "see quote above," accessed June 2020, https://www.brainyquote.com/quotes/benjamin_disraeli_401327.
131   von Goethe, "see quote above," accessed June 2020, https://www.passiton.com/inspirational-quotes/6881-whatever-you-can-do-or-dream-you-can-begin-it.
132   Rochefoucauld, "see quote above," accessed June 2020, https://www.bubo-quote.com/en/quote/2597-la-rochefoucauld-we-all-have-enough-strength-to-endure-the-misfortunes-of-others.

- If the wind will not serve, take to the oars. - Latin Proverb[133]
- Happy he who learns to bear what he cannot change. - Friedrich Schiller, German poet[134]
- Learn to let go. That is the key to happiness. - Buddha, Philosopher[135]
- Happiness resides not in possessions, and not in gold, happiness dwells in the soul. -Democritus, Greek philosopher[136]
- Life is the art of drawing sufficient conclusions from insufficient premises - Samuel Butler, British poet[137] They that apply themselves to trifling matters commonly become incapable of great ones. - Francois de la Rochefoucauld, French writer and memoirist[138]
- **There are times when we must deal with what is. - Gregory B. Davis**
- I ask not for a lighter burden, but for broader shoulders. - Jewish Proverb[139]

---

133   Latin Proverb, "see quote above," accessed June 2020, https://motivated-quotes.com/if-the-wind-will-not-serve-take-to-the-oars-latin-proverb/.

134   Schiller, "see quote above," accessed June 2020, https://www.treasurequotes.com/quotes/happy-he-who-learns-to-bear-what-he-cannot-cha.

135   Buddha, "see quote above," accessed June 2020, https://www.purelovequotes.com/author/buddha/learn-to-let-go-that-is-the-key-to-happiness/.

136   Democritus, "see quote above," accessed June 2020, https://www.goodreads.com/quotes/4808070-happiness-resides-not-in-possessions-and-not-in-gold-the.

137   Butler, "see quote above," accessed June 2020, https://www.forbes.com/quotes/8312/.

138   Rochefoucauld, "see quote above," accessed June 2020, https://www.quotetab.com/quotes/by-francois-de-la-rochefoucauld/8.

139   Jewish Proverb, "see quote above," accessed June 2020, https://quotefancy.

Life is Inharmonic: It will take more than you think

- Success depends upon previous preparation and without such preparation there is sure to be failure. - Confucius, Chinese Philosopher[140]
- Without continual growth and progress, such words as improvement, achievement and success have no meaning. - Benjamin Franklin, founding father of US Declaration of Independence[141]
- What is not started today is never finished tomorrow. - Johann Wolfgang von Goethe, German poet[142]
- The first step, my son, which one makes in the world, is the one on which depends the rest of our days. - Voltaire, French writer[143]
- The best time to plant a tree was 20 years ago. The second best time is now. - Chinese proverb[144]
- It is not easy, but it is worth it. - Unknown

com/quote/756883/Jewish-Proverb-I-ask-not-for-a-lighter-burden-but-for-broader-shoulders.

140   Confucius, "see quote above," accessed June 2020, https://quotefancy.com/quote/757699/Confucius-Success-depends-upon-previous-preparation-and-without-such-preparation-there-is.

141   Franklin, "see quote above," accessed June 2020, https://allauthor.com/quotes/34073/.

142   von Goethe, "see quote above," accessed June 2020, https://www.goodreads.com/quotes/8909081-what-is-not-started-today-is-never-finished-tomorrow.

143   Voltaire, "see quote above," accessed June 2020, https://www.forbes.com/quotes/9485/.

144   Chinese Proverb, "see quote above," accessed June 2020, https://www.psychologytoday.com/us/blog/joy-and-pain/201504/the-best-time-plant-tree-was-20-years-ago-no-matter.

- On all the peaks lies peace. - Johann Wolfgang von Goethe, German poet[145]

Life is Inharmonic: Being Alone

- You already have the world's most advanced creation: your mind. Use it to create your own miracles. - Atticus, Ancient philosopher[146]
- To dare to live alone is the rarest courage; since there are many who had rather meet their bitterest enemy in the field, than their own hearts in their closet. - Charles Caleb Colton, English writer[147]
- All men's misfortunes spring from their hatred of being alone. - Jean de la Bruyère, French satiric moralist[148]
- True happiness... Arises, in the first place from the enjoyment of one's self. - Joseph Addison, English essayist and poet[149]
- **Being alone is the best vitamin for the soul. - Gregory B. Davis**

145   von Goethe, "see quote above," accessed June 2020, https://www.buboquote.com/en/quote/2753-goethe-on-all-the-peaks-lies-peace.

146   Atticus, "see quote above," accessed June 2020, https://brandongaille.com/40-captivating-atticus-aristotle-quotes/.

147   Colton, "see quote above," accessed June 2020, https://www.brainyquote.com/quotes/charles_caleb_colton_101744.

148   Bruyère, "see quote above," accessed June 2020, https://allauthor.com/quotes/50746/.

149   Addison, "see quote above," accessed June 2020, https://www.goodreads.com/quotes/31303-true-happiness-is-of-a-retired-nature-and-an-enemy.

- What progress, you ask, have I made? I have begun to be a friend to myself. - Seneca, Roman Philosopher[150]
- **The more we love ourselves, the easier it is to love others. - Mary & Joe Davis**
- **You are alone because you choose to feel that way. - Gregory B. Davis**
- The secret of happiness, you see, is not found in seeking more, but in developing the capacity to enjoy less. - Socrates, Greek philosopher[151]

Life is Inharmonic: Sadness

- My life is a struggle. - Voltaire, French writer[152]
- **Be emotionally honest with yourself. - Gregory B. Davis**
- Good humor is the health of the soul, sadness is its poison. - Philip Stanhope, 4th Earl of Chesterfield, British statesman[153]
- Life is a series of natural and spontaneous changes. Don't resist them—that only creates sorrow. Let reality be reality. Let things flow naturally forward

---

150   Seneca, "see quote above," accessed June 2020, https://www.goodreads.com/quotes/8437426-what-progress-you-ask-have-i-made-i-have-begun.

151   Socrates, "see quote above," accessed June 2020, https://www.businessinsider.com/12-philosophers-share-quotes-on-happiness-2016-5#:~:text=%-22The%20secret%20of%20happiness%2C%20you,Socrates%2C%20lived%20in%20450%20BC.&text=For%20Socrates%2C%20one%20of%20the,from%20external%20rewards%20or%20accolades..

152   Voltaire, "see quote above," accessed June 2020, https://allauthor.com/quotes/141130/.

153   Stanhope, "see quote above," accessed June 2020, https://www.quotemaster.org/q5fe9e469473c22776be9353f47cd4f14.

in whatever way they like. - Lao Tzu, Chinese philosopher[154]

- Nothing is miserable unless you think it so; and on the other hand, nothing brings happiness unless you are content with it. - Boethius, Roman philosopher[155]

- Sadness flies away on the wings of time. - Jean de la Fontaine, French poet[156]

  You cannot prevent the birds of sadness from passing over your head, but you can prevent their making a nest in your hair. - Chinese Proverb[157]

- Reject your sense of injury and the injury itself disappears. - Marcus Aurelius, Roman leader[158]

- **Your choice of a life time get better or not. - Gregory B. Davis**

- Sadness does not come from bad circumstances. It comes from bad thoughts. - Unknown[159]

---

154   Lao Tzu, "see quote above," accessed June 2020, https://sophia.smith.edu/blog/wordsofwisdom/2011/03/15/life-is-a-series-of-natural-and-spontaneous-changes-dont-resist-them-that-only-creates-sorrow-let-reality-be-reality-let-things-flow-naturally-forward-in-whatever-way-they-like/.

155   Boethius, "see quote above," accessed June 2020, https://www.goodreads.com/quotes/76980-nothing-is-miserable-unless-you-think-it-so-and-on.

156   Fontaine, "see quote above," accessed June 2020, https://www.goodreads.com/quotes/111647-sadness-flies-away-on-the-wings-of-time.

157   Chinese Proverb, "see quote above," accessed June 2020, https://www.goodreads.com/quotes/243520-a-chinese-proverb-reminds-us-you-cannot-prevent-birds-of.

158   Aurelius, "see quote above," accessed June 2020, https://www.goodreads.com/quotes/74107-reject-your-sense-of-injury-and-the-injury-itself-disappears.

159   Unknown, "see quote above," accessed June 2020, https://scatteredquotes.com/sadness-not-come-from-circumstances/.

- **You can't carry garbage around and smell like a rose. - Gregory B. Davis**
- The only way to deal with an unfree world is to become so absolutely free that your very existence is an act of rebellion. - Albert Camus, French philosopher[160]

Discouragement

- It's not what happens to you, but how you react to it that matters. - Epictetus, Greek philosopher[161]
- Don't judge each day by the harvest you reap but by the seeds that you plant. - Robert Louis Stevenson, Scottish writer[162]
- Dream no small dreams for they have no power to move the hearts of men. - Johann Wolfgang von Goethe, German poet[163]
- There is no education like adversity. - Benjamin Disraeli, British politician, novelist, and essayist, serving twice as Prime Minister of the United Kingdom[164]

---

160   Camus, "see quote above," accessed June 2020, https://www.goodreads.com/quotes/114850-the-only-way-to-deal-with-an-unfree-world-is.
161   Epictetus, "see quote above," accessed June 2020, https://www.getselfhelp.co.uk//epictetus.htm.
162   Steveson, "see quote above," accessed June 2020, https://quotationcelebration.wordpress.com/2016/12/12/dont-judge-each-day-by-the-harvest-you-reap-but-by-the-seeds-that-you-plant-robert-louis-stevenson/.
163   von Goethe, "see quote above," accessed June 2020, https://www.quotes.net/quote/1153.
164   Disraeli, "see quote above," accessed June 2020, https://en.wikiquote.org/wiki/Benjamin_Disraeli.

- Fresh activity is the only means of overcoming adversity. - Johann Wolfgang von Goethe, German poet[165]
- There are two things a person should never be angry at, what they can help, and what they cannot. - Plato, Greek philosopher[166]
- If you can't catch fish, don't blame the sea. - Greek Proverb[167]
- Is life not a thousand times too short for us to bore ourselves? - Friedrich Nietzsche, German philosopher[168]
- **What we are now is not as important as what we may become. - Gregory B. Davis**
- He who has not the spirit of this age, has all the misery of it. - Voltaire, French writer[169]
- It doesn't matter how slowly you go as long as you do not stop. - Confucius, Chinese Philosopher[170]
- Every one goes astray, but the least imprudent are they who repent the soonest. - Voltaire, French writer[171]

---

165   von Goethe, "see quote above," accessed June 2020, http://quotetab.com/quote/by-johann-wolfgang-von-goethe/fresh-activity-is-the-only-means-of-over-coming-adversity.

166   Plato, "see quote above," accessed June 2020, https://www.lifehack.org/articles/communication/two-things-person-never-angry-can-help-plato.html.

167   Greek Proverb, "see quote above," accessed June 2020, https://www.goodreads.com/quotes/1254423-if-you-cannot-catch-a-fish-do-not-blame-the.

168   Nietzche, "see quote above," accessed June 2020, https://www.goodnews-network.org/nietzsche-quote-on-boredom/.

169   Voltaire, "see quote above," accessed June 2020, https://wise-quote.com/Francois-Voltaire-9657.

170   Confucius, "see quote above," accessed June 2020, https://www.quotespe-dia.org/authors/c/confucius/it-does-not-matter-how-slowly-you-go-as-long-as-you-do-not-stop-confucius/.

171   Voltaire, "see quote above," accessed June 2020, https://www.allgreatquo-tes.com/quote-468875/.

- It is during our darkest moments that we must focus to see the light. - Aristotle, Ancient Greek philosopher[172]
- All life is an experiment. The more experiments you make the better. - Ralph Waldo Emerson, American writer[173]
- **Even when discouraged, you are strong. - Gregory B. Davis**
- Plunge boldly into the thick of life, and seize where you will, it is always interesting. - Johann Wolfgang von Goethe, German poet[174]
- Perfect courage is to do without witnesses what one would be capable of doing with the world looking on.- Francois de la Rochefoucauld, French writer and memoirist[175]

Death

- There is a joy in sorrow which none but a mourner can know. - Jean Paul, German author[176]

---

172   Aristotle, "see quote above," accessed June 2020, https://www.mrgreatmotivation.com/2018/05/it-is-during-our-darkest-moments-that.html.

173   Emerson, "see quote above," accessed June 2020, http://www.quotationspage.com/quote/2547.html.

174   von Goethe, "see quote above," accessed June 2020, https://www.azquotes.com/quote/111888.

175   Rothefoucauld, "see quote above," accessed June 2020, http://www.inspiration.rightattitudes.com/authors/francois-de-la-rochefoucauld/.

176   Paul, "see quote above," accessed June 2020, https://allauthor.com/quotes/134394/.

- Don't cry because it is over, smile because it happened. - Ludwig Jacobowski, German poet[177]
- On neither the sun, nor death, can a man look fixedly. - Francois de la Rochefoucauld, French writer and memoirist[178]
- If you realize that all things change, there is nothing you will try to hold on to. If you are not afraid of dying, there is nothing you cannot achieve. - Lao Tzu, Chinese philosopher[179]
- It is vain for the coward to flee; death follows close behind; it is only by defying it that the brave escape. - Voltaire, French writer[180]
- Nothing is worth more than this day. You cannot relive yesterday. Tomorrow is still beyond your reach. - Johann Wolfgang von Goethe, German poet[181]
- **Life is over, start living. - Gregory B. Davis**
- The most happy man is he who knows how to bring into relation the end and beginning of his life. - Johann Wolfgang von Goethe, German poet[182]

---

177   Jacobowski, "see quote above," accessed June 2020, https://www.treasure-quotes.com/quotes/dont-cry-because-its-over-smile-because-it.

178   Rothefoucauld, "see quote above," accessed June 2020, https://www.allgreatquotes.com/quote-145446/.

179   Lao Tzu, "see quote above," accessed June 2020, https://www.goodreads.com/quotes/626677-if-you-realize-that-all-things-change-there-is-nothing.

180   Voltaire, "see quote above," accessed June 2020, https://www.buboquote.com/en/quote/2068-voltaire-it-is-vain-for-the-coward-to-flee-death-follows-clo-se-behind-it-is-only-by-defying-it.

181   von Goethe, "see quote above," accessed June 2020, https://www.goalcast.com/2019/04/02/johann-wolfgang-von-goethe-quotes/.

182   von Goethe, "see quote above," accessed June 2020, https://www.quotetab.com/johann-wolfgang-von-goethe-quotes-about-happiness.

- I would rather die of passion than of boredom. - Emile Zola, French novelist[183]
- Death may be the greatest of all human blessings. - Socrates, Greek philosopher[184]

Conclusion

- The greatest discovery of my generation is that a human being can alter his life by altering his attitudes. - William James, American philosopher[185]
- To find yourself, think for yourself. - Atticus, Ancient philosopher[186]
- Is there anyone so wise as to learn by the experience of others? - Voltaire, French writer[187]

---

183   Zola, "see quote above," accessed June 2020, https://quotecatalog.com/quote/emile-zola-i-would-rather-Z729m21/.

184   Socrates, "see quote above," accessed June 2020, https://www.brainyquote.com/quotes/socrates_378499.

185   James, "see quote above," accessed June 2020, http://clevelandbanner.com/stories/attitudes-not-aptitudes-control-our-lives-in-full,43268.

186   Atticus, "see quote above," accessed June 2020, https://www.goodreads.com/quotes/984262-to-find-yourself-think-for-yourself.

187   Voltarie, "see quote above," accessed June 2020, http://quoteseed.com/quotes/voltaire/voltaire-is-there-anyone-so-wise-as-to-learn-by/

www.ingramcontent.com/pod-product-compliance
Lightning Source LLC
LaVergne TN
LVHW051400080426
835508LV00022B/2912